Scottish Fold Cat

From bringing your kitten home to comforting your senior age companion

Scottish Fold Cat book including facts, price, personality, rescue, breeding, adoption, daily care, health, lifespan, how to find kittens for sale, and much more.

By

Alex Warrington, Ph.D.

and

Asia Moore

About the Authors

Alex Warrington, Ph.D. grew up on a farm with lots of animals (including cats, dogs, pigs, pigeons and chickens), where he developed a real passion for animals. He studied Chemical Engineering and obtained a Ph.D. from Imperial College in London.

Though Alex has been practicing his technical profession for many years, his real passion is caring for his pets that he keeps in his countryside house. He has shared most of his life with his animal friends and finds great pleasure and satisfaction in sharing his knowledge, expertise and enthusiasm through his informative pet books.

Asia Moore is an animal lover, groomer, professional Cynologist, Felinologist, Dog Whisperer and experienced Author who grew up on a farm with many different animals who were all her childhood teachers. She has written several hundred pet books, rescued many homeless cats in Canada and the United States, re-integrated feral cats into society and lived with many different feline and canine friends during her lifetime.

Asia also trains humans and rehabilitates felines, canines and other animals that have developed behavioral issues, so that everyone can live a happy and stress-free life together.

Asia lives in Canada, on Vancouver Island, off the west coast of British Columbia, and believes that with diligent research and the right training, all humans and animals can live together in peaceful harmony.

Visit Asia online at the following locations:
www.KnowsToNose.com
www.MustHavePublishing.com

Foreword

I have been a crazy cat lover for all of my life, beginning with a grey, Persian type cat named "Puss", when I was a young child growing up on a 30-acre hobby farm.

Over the years, I have shared my life with many different feline friends in several different countries, that just seemed to find me or follow me home and decided to stay.

I have many wonderful memories and stories of cats I've shared my life with and the following are just three that stand out in my mind.

When I lived in Scotland for two years, I adopted two kittens from a litter of orange tabbies, which I named *"Charlie"* and *"Lucy"* and after leash training them, they went walking with me along Buckingham Terrace every day. These two cats travelled back to Canada with me and became part of a household of cats that eventually grew as large as seven.

Once, I moved into a house and quickly discovered that there was a feral cat, named "Wharf", living in the back yard. The former house renters, who apparently couldn't catch him when they were moving out, had sadly abandoned this shorthaired, white cat. While it took me some time and plenty of patience, I finally won this cat over, one back stair at a time (where I left his food and water); once he trusted me, Wharf decided it was safe to come inside and he became a happy house cat.

Another time, when I was vacationing on Maui in Hawaii, I found two starving, feral kittens (one white and one orange, which I named *"Coco"* and *"Mango")* hiding under a bush and secretly took them into my condo. These two frightened kittens pretty much lived behind the couch for two weeks, only venturing out from their perceived safe zone to eat and drink.

Before I was to head back home, I found a mobile vet who provided me with a travel crate and had the kittens vaccinated before they experienced their first plane ride at about 10 weeks of age as I brought them back to the west coast of Canada where they soon joined ranks with the rest of my feline crew.

The most interesting part of this story is that my Siamese seal point male (named "Nano") that was staying with friends while I was in

Maui, was very closely bonded with me, and I was worried he would be extremely jealous when I returned with two strange kittens.

Amazingly, Nano actually took these two kittens under his whiskers and immediately mothered and showed them the feline ropes as they grew up in Canada, and they remained best pals for their entire lives.

I feel so fortunate to have the opportunity to share my feline passion and experience with you through writing books that will help you have the best life with your feline friend. All the cats that have wandered through my past have brought me so much joy and I believe that this book will help you make the best decisions for all stages of your cat's life and equally enjoy your journey together.

^..^ Asia Moore

Felinologist, Cat Lover and Dog Whisperer

Table of Contents

Chapter 1: Introduction

It's important to gather as much information as possible before you take the plunge to share your home with a furry friend.

While humans and cats have been co-habiting for more than 10,000 years, you will want to choose the feline companion that is best suited for you and your family.

The Scottish Fold Full Lifecycle Care Guide is designed to answer the questions you may have when researching this intelligent purebred feline. If you are considering sharing your home with the medium-sized, affectionate and playful Scottish Fold, this manual is for you.

Learn all about this adaptable and placid cat breed, including facts and interesting tidbits and how to care for every stage of this feline's life.

This book contains all the information you need, from choosing a breeder and finding the perfect kitten, to how to care for your cat during their senior years.

In addition, you will learn about transitioning through litter box training, daily care, health problems inherent in the breed, feeding, grooming and house rules as well as the end of their life, so that you can make an educated decision when deciding whether or not the playful and intelligent Scottish Fold cat is the right choice for you and your family.

Chapter 2: What is a Scottish Fold Cat?

The medium-sized Scottish Fold can have many different coat colors and patterns. Either long or shorthaired, the distinctive, forward pointing folded ear (resulting from a genetic mutation) accentuates the rounded head and makes them look very "owlish".

As a kitten, the Scottish Fold is born with normal, pointy ears, which don't begin to fold until the kittens are about two to four weeks old. Some of them may continue to retain normal, pointy ears and these kittens are called "straights".

This cat's ears didn't always fold quite so dramatically as they do today. However, with human intervention and decades of selective breeding, the modern Scottish Fold often has ears that lie completely flat against the head.

Because of the Governing Council of the Cat Fancy (GCCF) that were concerned about showing cats with physical deformities that might have ear problems, these cats are no longer registered with this United Kingdom organisation and are no longer shown in Europe.

This very quiet cat has a soft voice and is known for adopting comical poses, such as sleeping on their back or sitting in the *"Buddha"* position, stretched out with their paws on the belly..

The Scottish Fold is usually an affectionate, easy-going cat with a gentle disposition that will be relaxed around the family dog, other cats and children and will want to spend plenty of time in the company of their humans. This makes them a smart choice for families with children and other pets.

This intelligent cat likes games and activities and does not particularly enjoy spending a lot of time alone, although they do like exploring outdoors.

The Scottish Fold is an adaptable cat that can easily fit into the changing dynamics of a busy multi-pet, large family household.

This *"owl in a cat suit"* was originally called *"lop-eared"*, after the lop-eared rabbit, and longhaired varieties are often referred to as *"Highland Folds"*.

The Scottish Fold is usually a healthy cat with a sweet "purrsonality" that will be friendly with family, children, dogs, other pets and strangers.

If this will be an indoor cat, you will need to take the time to play with them every day, because not only will this keep them happy and physically healthy, but it will also help to curb the tendency for an indoor cat to become overweight.

1. History of the Scottish Fold Cat

While the true origins of many feline breeds can be difficult to trace, the Scottish Fold cat can follow their origins back to one mutation in an otherwise seemingly ordinary cat that occurred naturally and unexpectedly in a white cat named Susie.

Susie, who was born with unusually folded ears, kept control of the mouse population in a barn in the Tayside region of Scotland. Interestingly, this "new breed" might have escaped notice had this barn feline not been seen by a shepherd with an interest in cats.

During the early 1960's, William Ross noticed the unusual Susie and when she had a litter of kittens, Ross acquired a female, which he named *"Snooks"* and thus began the development of a new cat breed.

Ross originally named this new breed "lop-eared cats", until this sweet and loving cat later became known as the "Scottish Fold" to better represent their country of origin.

The gene mutation that causes the folded ears in these cats is dominant, which means that if either parent has the gene, the resulting kittens can also have folded ears.

While still not a recognized breed in their country of origin, these cats were imported into the United States in the early 1970's and within a few short years had been recognized by many different associations, including:

- The International Cat Association (TICA), one of the fastest growing genetic cat registries, recognizing 71 different breeds;

- The Scottish Fold is the 7th most popular breed registered with The Cat Fanciers' Association (CFA), established in the United States in 1906. This is the largest pedigreed cat registry in the world, recognizing 42 separate breeds; and

- The American Cat Fanciers' Association (ACFA), originating in 1955, and known as the *"Fairest, Friendliest and Most Fun feline association whose goal is to promote the welfare, education, knowledge and interest in all domesticated, purebred and non-purebred cats".*

2. Little Known Cat Facts and Cat Secrets

There are many interesting and unknown secrets and facts concerning the world of felines (and the Scottish Fold cat in particular), that anyone thinking about sharing their life with a cat will want to know, and the following are a few you may find enlightening:

1) The word *"cat"* is an Old English word originally spelled *"catt"*, having its source in the Late Latin word *"catus"*, meaning *"domestic cat"*, which likely comes from the Afro-Asiatic word *"kaddîska"*, meaning *"wild cat"*.

2) A cat coat contains up to 130,000 hairs per square inch, and the surface area of a single cat, if you include all of its hair, is roughly the same as the surface area of a Ping-Pong table.

3) What actually causes many people to be allergic to cats is not their fur, but rather an adhesive protein found on cat skin called *"Fel d 1."* There is no such thing as a "hypoallergenic" cat (even hairless ones), because while they may produce less of this protein, all cats produce it.

4) Everyone believes that cats purr when they are happy, however, they may also purr for other reasons. For instance, researchers believe that cats may purr when hungry or as a means of self - soothing during stressful situations.

5) Scientists have learned that cats purr at a range that promotes tissue regeneration (a frequency of 26 Hertz), which means that purring may play a significant role in maintaining the health of our cat's bones.

6) Many people squirt water or yell at their cat when he or she chooses to sharpen their claws on the corner of their favorite couch. Guess what?
   To a cat, your squirting behavior is simply frustrating and 100% crazy because a cat's scratching is only a natural feline instinct. Instead, provide your cat with a scratching post that is more enticing that your couch.

7) While cats have a 200-degree visual field, as opposed to the 180-degree that we humans see, their longer distance visual acuity isn't as good as humans, who can see sharp images as far away as 200 feet (60 metre), while object farther away than 20 feet (6 metre) might appear blurry to a cat.

8) Cats can see much better than humans in dim light, because their eyes contain many more rod cells, which are responsible for night vision acuity, and may explain why cats become more active and love to hunt at nighttime.

9) While there is no denying that cats simply love boxes, there are many theories why this is the case.
   Maybe they feel comfortable and secure in small spaces, or because they like small hiding places where they can de-stress, or because they prefer to run from a conflicting situation and

locate themselves in a safe zone that might be represented by the box, or simply because cats like warm spaces where they can curl up to preserve their body heat.

10) Some cats like to be petted – some do not, so be careful not to inflict petting on your cat who doesn't really enjoy it, because this can elevate your cat's stress level, which can lead to behavioral and health problems.

11) A brain-controlling parasite called *"Toxoplasma gondii"* that can be transmitted by cats to humans is thought to cause psychotic behavior, and researchers in the United Kingdom believe that cats are infecting more than 1,000 humans with this parasite every day.

12) There was a study comparing the personality and psychology of our domestic cats with larger wild cats carried out at the University of Edinburgh in Scotland indicating that our house cats have much in common with African lions, and as such have a *"high inclination toward dominance, impulsiveness and neuroticism"*.

Some researchers believe that we are inviting little predators into our homes and that… *"If they were bigger, they would probably kill you"*.

13) In the United States, 12,000 people are hospitalized every year after being tripped by their cat.

14) In Talkeetna, Alaska, a cat named Stubbs has been mayor for 15 years.

15) A group of more than two cats is called a *"clowder"* or a *"clutter"*, *"a glaring"*, or *"a pounce"*, while a group of kittens can be called *"a kindle"*, *"a litter"*, or *"an intrigue"*.

16) A group of wild felines is called a *"dowt"* or a *"destruction"*.

17) A non-spayed pregnant female cat is called a *"Queen"* and a common term for a female cat is a *"molly"*.

18) When a female cat gives birth to her kittens, this is called *"kindling"* and this term also refers to rabbits giving birth.

19) You probably know that a non-neutered male cat is called a *"tom"* or *"tomcat"*, but did you know that a neutered male cat is called a *"gib"*?

20) There are approximately 40 recognized breeds of cats worldwide and more than 500 million domestic cats.

21) When cats grimace, they are usually scent-tasting the air.

22) Cats rub against people, other pets and objects not only to be affectionate, but also to mark their territory because there are scent glands around the cat face (as well as their paws and tail area).

23) An average-sized litter of kittens is anywhere between one and five kittens, with the largest known litter being 19 kittens (15 survived).

24) During the times of ancient Egypt (when cats were highly worshipped), to be caught smuggling a cat out of Egypt was punishable by death.

25) It is now believed that the domestic cat has been around since 3600 B.C. or 2,000 years before Egyptian pharaohs.

26) Most cats can jump up to five times their own height and have no collarbone, so they can fit through spaces the size of their head.

27) The Egyptian Mau is the oldest and fastest breed of cat – Mau is the Egyptian word for "cat".

28) A cat's hearing is their best sense – they have the ability to hear sounds over three times higher than humans at 64 kHz.

29) Female cats are typically right-pawed, while many male cats are typically left-pawed.

30) Cat whiskers tend to grow as long as the width of their body.

31) Many cats are lactose intolerant, so be careful you are not making your cat sick by feeding them dairy products.

32) It is believed that the name *"tabby"*, in reference to striped cats, originated in a neighborhood in Baghdad, Iraq, called *"Attabiyah"*, because their striped coats were reminiscent of the wavy patterns produced in the silk that was manufactured in this city.

33) While most cats hate swimming or getting wet, because their coats cannot insulate them from the cold when they are wet, a cat called the *"Turkish Van"* (bred in central Asia) enjoys swimming because this cat's coat has a unique, water-resistant texture.

34) The reason why cats are attracted to the aromatic "catnip" herb (also called catmint or cats' plant) is because it releases the chemical *"nepetalactone"* that mimics the smell of a cat pheromone. Two other plants (Silver Vine and Valerian) also have the same effect as catnip on many cats.

35) While everyone knows that cats spend a lot of their day sleeping, on average a cat will spend 2/3rds of every day asleep, which means that a 9-year-old cat has been awake for only 3 years of his or her life.

36) Did you know that the immensely convenient and popular *"cat flap"* door was invented by Sir Isaac Newton to solve a problem he had when his cat kept opening the door in a room where he was carrying out an experiment that required darkness?

37) We all know that coffee is an expensive industry, however, you may not know that the world's most expensive and rarest coffee, called *"Kopi Luwak"* (from Indonesia) is created by civet cats. Apparently the cat ingests the coffee berries, which pass out through the colon, to then be harvested, cleaned, roasted and sold to coffee connoisseurs for approximately $500 (£363) for a 1-pound (450 gram) bag (think I'll pass).

38) The fancy Greek name for a person who is a "cat lover" or has a liking or fondness for cats, while definitely Greek to most of us non-Greek speaking humans is *"Ailurophilia"*.

39) Until we humans started meddling in the breeding of cats, and fashion dictated longer coats, approximately 100 years ago, most cats had short- haired coats.

40) While many healthy cats can live to be 20 years of age, apparently the oldest cat on record was a cat living in Austin, Texas, named Crème Puff, who died three days after her 38th birthday.

41) Cats sweat only through their paws.

42) In the cat world (both large and small), the cheetah is the only cat that does not sheath its claws when at rest.

43) While humans only have 6 muscles in the outer ear, cats have 32, which means that a cat can rotate his or her ears 180 degrees.

44) Cats can make approximately 100 different sounds (as opposed to the 10 sounds that dogs can make).

45) Over short distances, a cat can run at speeds up to 31 mph (49 km/h).

46) The city of Rome has more homeless cats than any other city in the world.

47) While unthinkable in most parts of the world, in certain parts of Asia, such as southern China, cats are looked upon as a source of food where it is estimated that every day approximately 10,000 cats are consumed.

48) There could be as many as 60 million wild (feral) cats in the United States.

49) In stark contrast to the dog world, cats have not had to endure major changes as a result of hybrid breeding experimentation throughout their lengthy domestication period.

50) There is a legend that says Mohammed so loved his cats that he used to rest his hand on their head, and that this is why the tabby cat has a distinctive "M" on their heads.

51) It is said that President Bill Clinton's cat (Socks) received more letters to the White House than the President himself.

52) One of the reasons that the cat is so flexible is because they have up to 53 loosely fitting vertebrae – humans only have 34.

53) As a result of their hunting prowess, cats have driven 33 or more species to extinction.

54) A cat's heart beats almost twice as fast as a human heart (110 to 140 beats per minute).

55) As a result of cats being extremely sensitive to vibrations, many believe that they have the ability to detect earthquake tremors 10 to 15 minutes before humans.

56) The dominant gene that produces the folded ears in the Scottish Fold cat may also cause a degenerative joint disease and in order to avoid this problem, breeders are encouraged to mate straight-eared to folded-eared cats.

57) While the Scottish Fold is typically seen with copper colored eyes, their eyes can be any color.

58) The Scottish Fold cat is nicknamed *"lop-eared", "owls in cat suits", "Highland Folds"*, or simply *"Folds"*.

3. The Different Types and Colors of Scottish Fold Cats

Accepted by all North American cat registries, the Scottish Fold Cat is a highly popular breed, recognized with many different shaded, solid, bi-color, color point and patterned coat colors, including:

- Black Smoke Scottish Fold Cat
- Black Smoke Tortoiseshell Scottish Fold Cat
- Blue Scottish Fold Cat
- Blue Cream Shaded Scottish Fold Cat
- Blue Cream Smoke Scottish Fold Cat
- Blue Eyed White Scottish Fold Cat
- Blue Patched Scottish Fold Cat
- Blue Patched Tabby Scottish Fold Cat
- Blue Silver Patched Tabby Scottish Fold Cat
- Blue Silver Tabby Scottish Fold Cat
- Blue Smoke Scottish Fold Cat
- Blue Tabby Scottish Fold Cat
- Brown Tabby Scottish Fold Cat
- Brown Patched Tabby Scottish Fold Cat
- Cameo Scottish Fold Cat
- Chinchilla Scottish Fold Cat
- Chocolate Shaded Scottish Fold Cat
- Copper Eyed White Scottish Fold Cat
- Cream Scottish Fold Cat
- Cream Tabby Scottish Fold Cat
- Golden Scottish Fold Cat
- Golden Chinchilla Scottish Fold Cat
- Golden Patched Tabby Scottish Fold Cat
- Golden Tabby Scottish Fold Cat
- Grey Scottish Fold Cat
- Red Scottish Fold Cat
- Shaded Cameo Scottish Fold Cat
- Shaded Silver Scottish Fold Cat
- Shell Cameo Scottish Fold Cat
- Silver Scottish Fold Cat
- Silver Patched Tabby Scottish Fold Cat
- Silver Tabby Scottish Fold Cat

- Smoke Cameo Scottish Fold Cat
- Spotted Tabby Scottish Fold Cat
- Tortoiseshell Scottish Fold Cat
- White Scottish Fold Cat
- Long Haired Scottish Fold Cat

4. Scottish Fold Cat Names

Need help choosing a name for your Scottish Fold cat? Think about their round heads, flattened ears, compelling, large, round eyes, and their resemblance to owls or teddy bears, and you'll soon come up with many appropriate names for your cat or kitten. Here are a few suggestions to get you started:

- Buttons
- Cloche
- Hooty
- Peaches
- Pumpkin
- Scotty
- Teddy

The charming Scottish Fold is a medium-sized cat that can have a short, medium or long coat. They have beautiful, large round eyes that while typically copper in color, depending on the coat color and pattern, can be blue, gold, green, hazel and sometimes *"odd-eyed"*, which means the eyes are two different colors.

Every cat, no matter what his or her pedigree might be, will have a unique personality to share with their human counterparts, and being a good guardian means that we need to listen to our fur friends.

For instance, our cats *"tell"* us when they are unhappy, when they are bored, when they are hungry, when they are under-exercised or want attention from their humans, yet often we are too busy to pay attention, or we just think they are being badly behaved.

Many humans today are deciding to have pets (usually cats or dogs) instead of children and without the proper knowledge, not being well informed about the needs of our chosen furry companion can have a seriously detrimental effect upon the health and behavior of our feline companions.

In order to be the best guardians for our cats, it's important that we humans have a better understanding of what our feline friends need from us to be physically and mentally healthy, rather than what we need from them, so that they can live in safety and harmony within our human environment.

Sadly, many of us humans are not well equipped to give our cats what they really need and that is why so many homeless, abandoned and frustrated cats and kittens end up in the SPCA or at endless rescue facilities worldwide.

First and foremost, our cats need to be respected for their unique feline qualities and in order to create a harmonious relationship, we humans need to spend more time receiving the proper training so that we can learn how to do the best for our furry friends.

No matter the breed, any cat can enrich our human lives providing that we treat the cat well and understand what they need to live a safe and happy life, and this is a universal truth that applies to any cat, whether a purebred Scottish Fold cat or kitten or a rescued cat from the local Humane Society or SPCA.

It should be noted that, even though most of the information presented in this book refers specifically to the Scottish Fold cat, there may be some reference points that can be applied equally successfully to any cat breed.

Chapter 3: Choosing a Breeder

1. Locating a Scottish Fold Cat Breeder

Although a good breeder cannot guarantee the lifelong health of any kitten, they should easily be able to provide a prospective guardian with plenty of information about the health of the kitten's parents.

If you are considering becoming a prospective Scottish Fold cat guardian, you should definitely have a serious conversation with the breeder, so that you are clearly informed about exactly what health tests have been carried out and what the results revealed about the parents of a kitten you may be considering purchasing.

For instance, a reputable breeder will have had their breeding cats tested for problems inherent in the breed and prospective kitten purchasers should always inquire about possible congenital problems the parents or grandparents of the kitten might have, including any premature deaths.

2. Let's Meet the Parents

Meeting the mother and father of your new kitten can show and tell you a great deal about what the kittens might look like, plus what the temperament and demeanor of your kitten will likely be when they grow into adulthood.

While determining a kitten's personality or temperament when they are still in the care of their mother is only a small percentage of their potential as an adult cat, because training and socializing them after 8-10 weeks will be the responsibility of their new guardian, how they are raised during the first few weeks of their life is still very important.

A kitten's earliest days will be a combination of what they experience in their environment while they are in the breeder's care, what they learn from the mother cat and the other kittens in the litter and other animals they may experience, and the genes inherited from both parents.

Ideally, you will want to take the time to visit the breeder several times, so that you can observe the parent cats interact with the kittens and ask plenty of questions, all of which will help you to get a true feeling for the trustworthiness and sincerity of the breeder.

Do not underestimate how significant the early environment provided by the breeder and the parents of the kittens can be, as well as the later environment, socializing and training provided by the kitten's new guardian, because all of this can have a substantial effect on how well your kitten will ultimately behave as an adult cat.

Generally speaking, cats have excellent memories, which means that if their environment is less than ideal during their early developmental period, they may develop behavioral problems in later life.

The first 2 to 7 weeks of a kitten's life is the time when a baby cat will begin to memorize and develop "survival" skills, which will be very important for them as an adult cat.

Kittens learn their early skills by watching their mother and playing with their siblings and while play looks to us human simply like a lot of cute antics, play is highly important because it doesn't just help develop motor skills, coordination and hunting skills for later life, but this is also the time when the kitten will bond with other cats and learn their ranking within the litter and this will help to set their temperament as an adult cat.

Also, during this highly formative time in a young kitten's life it is very important that they experience pleasant human contact, otherwise they may learn to be forever distrustful of humans.

3. Questions to Ask a Breeder

Get to know your breeder by asking them why they decided to breed the Scottish Fold cat and how long they have been breeding. Ask if the breeder will permit you to visit their facility and if they will give you a tour.

Ask the breeder if they own both breeding parents, or if they do not, ask if they are familiar with or have worked closely with both parents of the kitten you may be considering.

Ask how often the breeder allows the females and males to breed and reproduce, and in a larger cattery operation, ask if the breeder will allow you to see the other cats in the kennel and take notice whether the cattery is clean, well maintained and animal friendly.

Will the breeder permit you to see other adult cats, or other kittens that the breeder owns, socialize together?

Pay attention to whether the breeder limits the amount of time that you are permitted to handle the kittens. A reputable breeder will be concerned for the safety and health of all their kittens and will only permit serious buyers to handle the kittens.

Check to find out if the breeder is registered or recognized by your local, state or national breed organization.

a) Medical Questions: every reputable breeder will certainly ensure that their kittens have received vaccinations and de-worming specific to the age of the kittens.

Always ask the breeder what shots the kitten has received and when it was last de-wormed and ask for the name of the breeder's veterinarian. If you discover that the breeder has not carried out any of these procedures or they are unable to tell you when the last shots or de-worming was carried out, look elsewhere.

Also ask to see the breeder's veterinarian report on the health of the kitten you may be interested in purchasing, and if they cannot produce this report, look elsewhere.

b) Temperament Questions: you will want to choose a kitten with a friendly, easy going and congenial temperament and your breeder should be able to help you with your selection.

A good breeder will have noticed personality and temperament traits very early on in their kittens and should be able to provide a prospective purchaser with valuable insight concerning each kitten's unique personality.

Also, ask the breeder about the temperament and personalities of the kitten's parents and ask what they have done to socialize the kittens. Ask how old the kittens must be before they can be taken to their new homes.

If the breeder is willing to let their kittens go any earlier than 8 to 10 weeks of age, they are more interested in making a profit than in the health of their kittens.

Always be certain to ask if a kitten you are interested in has displayed any signs of aggression or fear, because if this is happening at such an early age, you may experience on-going behavioral troubles when the kitten becomes older.

c) Guarantee Questions: a reputable breeder will be interested in the lifelong health and wellbeing of all of their kittens and good breeders will want you to call them should a problem arise at any time during the life of your kitten.

In addition, a good breeder will want you to return a kitten or cat to them if for some reason you are unable to continue to care for it, rather than seeing the cat go to a shelter or rescue facility.

If the breeder you are considering does not offer this type of return policy, find one who does, because no ethical breeder would ever permit a kitten from one of his or her litters to end up in a shelter.

d) Return Contract: reputable breeders offer return contracts. They do this to protect their reputation and to also make sure that a kitten they have sold that might display a genetic defect will not have the opportunity to breed and continue to spread the defect, which could weaken the entire breed.

Many breeders also offer return contracts because purchasing a kitten from a breeder can be an expensive proposition, and if you find out that the kitten has a worrisome genetic defect, this could cost you a great deal with respect to unexpected veterinarian care. In such cases, most honest and reputable breeders offer a return policy, and will be happy to give you another kitten.

e) Testimonials: ask the breeder you are considering to provide you with testimonials from some of their previous clients, and then actually contact those people to ask them about their experience with the breeder, and the health and temperament of their cat.

A good breeder has nothing to hide and will be more than happy to provide you with testimonials because their best recommendation is a happy customer.

f) Breeder Reputation: the Internet can be a valuable resource when researching the reputation of a breeder. For instance, you will be able to post on most forums discussing breeders to quickly find out what you need to know from those who have first-hand experience.

Be prepared to answer questions the breeder may have for you, because a reputable breeder will want to ask a prospective purchaser their own questions, so that they can satisfy themselves that you are going to be a good caretaker for their kitten.

First, do your homework about the breed you are considering and then carry out as much research as possible about the specific breeder you are considering before making your initial visit to their facility.

The more information you have gathered about the breed and the breeder you are considering, and the more information the breeder knows about you, the more successful the match will be.

Chapter 4: Scottish Fold Cat Statistics & Types

1. Country of Origin

Scotland is considered the country of origin for the Scottish Fold cat.

2. Litter Size

While more or less can be born, an average litter size will be 4 kittens.

3. Average Cat Size

While dependent on the cat's gender and breeding, when measured at the shoulder, the average Scottish Fold cat will be medium sized, and weigh between 6 and 13 pounds (2.7 and 5.8 kilograms) or more (depending on the size of both parents), with a tail length that is in proportion to the body length.

This cat has a well-padded, rounded body with medium to short legs, a short nose and a round, domed head resting on a short neck. Their large, broadly spaced eyes give the Scottish Fold a "sweet" expression.

4. Temperature & Heart Rate

Temperature: 100 to 102.5 degrees Fahrenheit (38 to 39.1 Celsius).

Respiratory Rate: 20 to 30 per minute.

Heart Rate: 140 to 220 per minute.

Gums: should be pink.

5. The Domestic Cat Lifespan

There are many factors that may play a role in how long your cat may live, including how well you care for them, whether they are an indoor or outdoor cat, and the particular cat breed.

However, the average domestic cat *("Felis catus")* will enter middle age by their 7th year, will be considered a senior cat by age 12, and *"geriatric"* by age 15.

Generally speaking, our cats are living longer lives, which means that while the "average" lifespan for a domestic house cat may be 10 to 16 years of age, many of our feline friends are living quite a bit longer, as a result of advances in nutrition and veterinary science, with some living into their late teens and early 20's.

The Scottish Fold lifespan is estimated to be approximately 15 years.

6. Coat Colors and Features

The unique Scottish Fold cat is noted for their forward folded ears, large, round, clear eyes and sweet personality.

Adult Coats: while there can be 75 or more different coat colors and patterns, similar to what is seen in other breeds, perhaps one of the most recognized Scottish Fold cat colors, is the short-haired grey or orange tabby with copper eyes. .

Daily Coat Care: will be very important throughout the life of your cat and this should begin when they are kittens, so that they do not fight the process for their entire life.

Get in the habit of spending a few minutes brushing your cat's coat each day to help remove dead hair, dirt and other debris and keep them looking their best.

The Scottish Fold, depending on their particular length of coat, will require more or less brushing in order to reduce moderate shedding and remove any burrs or other debris. Be aware that you may need to brush your cat more frequently during higher shedding seasons.

Brushing or combing is also a good time to spot any abnormalities before they become a health issue and you should also use this time to check his or her teeth and notice if your cat's nails require clipping.

Chapter 5: The Scottish Fold Cat Purrsonality

When you properly socialize your kitten or cat with different animals and people, depending on the individual cat and the energy of the other animals or strangers, this cat will usually be sociable.

Generally speaking, the Scottish Fold cat is a friendly, gentle and sweet-natured feline that will fit well into busy households with children and other pets.

They are usually happy to peacefully accept new circumstances that may change your life over the years. This curious and playful feline is an adaptable and affectionate cat that is at home in a rambling country estate, as he or she would be taking up residence in a modest city apartment.

Very playful and capable of learning tricks, this cat is interested in what is going on in their environment, and loves the attention he or she receives from children who are polite and respectful.

While playful, social and interactive with family members and other pets, this cat is still independent enough to enjoy spending short periods of time alone. An excellent mouser, they will also use their superior hunting skills to catch flies or other insects and pests that might find their way into your home.

The Scottish Fold is also usually very tolerant of other cats in the home as well as dogs and younger children that know how to be respectful of their space. If he or she is faced with too much rough treatment, rather than scratching or biting, he or she will most often quietly disappear and retreat to a safer location.

Depending on the particular cat, the docile and affectionate Scottish Fold may enjoy spending time purring in your lap or sitting quietly beside you. Smart and adaptable, this easy to train feline will quickly learn your house rules. Once you teach him or her that the couch is not their scratching post, they will be happy to sharpen their claws on a provided post or pad.

Always keep in mind that every cat will have a unique personality and depending upon their genetics and early upbringing, will react to strangers and unfamiliar circumstances each in his or her own way.

For instance, some cats love company and will happily greet strangers, while others may immediately seek out a safe hiding place when visitors come to call.

There are a few guidelines that you can use to help teach your visitors proper cat-greeting *"etiquette"* and help your cat feel more comfortable with delivery people and strangers visiting your home.

For instance, if your cat is acting overly cautious, just ask your visitors to simply ignore him or her and avoid eye contact. If the cat decides to approach, keep your energy calm and slowly extend your hand so he or she can smell you. Then if the cat seems interested, perhaps give a gentle head or neck scratch, while continuing to avoid eye contact.

Most cats will start to rub up against humans once they feel comfortable, so wait for the cat to signal that they may be agreeable to a gentle scratch and don't try to invade their space by pursuing them.

This will be especially important if you have young children visiting and if you are teaching your cat to be social, you will also need to teach the children a slow and calm approach.

You may also use a treat or an interactive toy to entice a cautious cat to approach, however, always stay calm and let the cat come to you.

It is imperative to properly socialize every cat, so that they learn basic house rules that will keep them safe and become safely integrated into your family, and you need to put in the effort to begin socialization when they are still young kittens so that they do not become overly fearful or skittish and spend all their time hiding under the bed when friends come to visit.

When you do take the time to socialize your kitten, you will help him or her grow up to be a self-confident and calm adult cat that will enjoy the company of humans and will happily interact with your family and friends.

All guardians need to be fully aware that a cat who does not receive early socialization may spend their lives living in fear of people and everything else they may encounter in their environment, which can include noises, unfamiliar humans, children, dogs, other cats and pets.

1. Behavior With Children and Other Pets

Generally speaking, when considering a cat companion for your family, and depending upon the age of your children (as younger children tend to be loud, boisterous and unpredictable), you will want to look for a cat that is social, not overly stressed by loud noises and fast movement, and that enjoys play time.

However, if your children are very young, you will have to protect both the kitten or cat from the children, and the children from the kitten or cat, as young kittens cannot protect themselves from rough handling and may become overly stressed and afraid, while an older cat may bite and scratch the toddlers to remove themselves from their grasp.

On the other hand, a family with older children, that are less inclined to be loud and boisterous, will want to find a lower-energy and more independent cat (perhaps a full grown rescue) that will not have the higher activity needs of a kitten or very young cat.

No matter the age of your children, when choosing a cat you will want one that is naturally friendly, affectionate, easy-going, that enjoys play and being petted, and can be trusted not to become overly agitated, bite or attack if they receive too much attention.

Generally, cats that have been born into an environment where there are children, other pets and animals will be the best kid-friendly candidates for integrating smoothly into a family setting, and the adaptable and friendly Scottish Fold is usually a placid and easy-going feline that will fit in very well.

While many smaller pets such as mice, rats and birds are the natural prey of the domestic cat, if they are raised with them, they can learn not to harm pet birds or smaller animals, although all cats are not to be totally trusted around mice or small birds.

2. Cats and Dogs

Despite the old myth that cats and dogs are sworn enemies, and while it's always best to introduce them to each other when they are young, these alleged antagonists get along together much more amicably than many might think.

According to a survey carried out at Tel Aviv University in Israel, where Neta-li Feuerstein and her graduate advisor (Joseph Terkel) surveyed 170 Israeli homes that housed both a pet cat and a pet dog, with research detailed in the journal *of "Applied Animal Behavior Science",* their results indicated that:

"...Two-thirds of the households reported an amicable relationship between the species. Indifference prevailed in a quarter, and less than a tenth reported fighting..."

Many of us humans who enjoy the company of both cats and dogs have plenty of first-hand experience strongly indicating that our canine and feline friends (in most cases) have been able to put their species differences aside as many form strong bonds of friendship and don't just tolerate one another, but enjoy playing and sleeping together.

3. Escaping Cats

All cats are natural athletes that can jump approximately five times their own height and will be superior at escaping confinement if given the opportunity, so make sure that if you plan to let them outside, your cat is safely contained within their own back yard.

Keep in mind that the cat is a natural hunter and will not hesitate to chase vermin or an interesting bird, which means they can quickly wander out of the immediate vicinity, which could mean crossing a busy street or being chased by a dog that thinks cats are prey.

They can certainly figure out how to escape from confinement and will use their strong legs to jump fences, climb fences, or find cracks or small spaces they can squeeze through if they want to get out, and they usually <u>will</u> want to get out because the grass is always greener further down the block and if they are not being entertained at home, they will seek adventure elsewhere.

Of course, all cats will have a much higher urge to roam before they are spayed or neutered, therefore, early spaying or neutering of a kitten will go a long way toward helping to curb any wanderlust tendencies that may be a result of raging hormones that are driving them to find mates.

Chapter 6: Before You Buy a Scottish Fold Cat

No matter what breed you may be considering as a possible candidate for sharing your home and life, this decision should never be entered into lightly.

Keep in mind that the reason many cats end up abandoned and behind bars at the local SPCA, Pound or Rescue facility is because the individual or family chose poorly when deciding to get a cat and after the kitten grew out of their cute phase, they found the burden of caring for the cat overwhelming.

This happens far more than you might imagine and the overflowing rescue facilities are a testament to how many cats have been poorly chosen.

Before you become another sad statistic, make sure you really are a good candidate for sharing your life with a cat.

Those who may be considering sharing their home with a Scottish Fold cat need to carry out research and make sure they have all the facts straight before taking the plunge, because there are always many important factors to keep in mind.

Currently, the Scottish Fold cat is a highly popular choice ", or very in style, and any time a cat or other animal acquires a "vogue" status, we humans become inspired and often rush to pursue the trend, so that we can also feel in vogue and keep up with the Joneses. Perhaps this is not the best reason to choose any particular breed.

Better is to be cautious about being influenced by trends and instead, carry out your own research, so that you are informed and thoroughly understand what to expect from a breed you are considering.

Consider that without clear thinking and understanding of the commitment level required by you and your family when bringing a cat into your home, you may end up contributing to the worldwide epidemic problem of overflowing shelters and rescue facilities.

Chapter 7: Breeders and Things to Consider in Advance

Once you've decided that the Scottish Fold cat is the right breed for you, you will then need to take the time to properly research quality breeders so that you can be confident that you will be bringing home a healthy kitten.

You will want to keep in mind that almost every responsible and reputable breeder will belong to the Cat Fanciers Association (CFA) and they will most likely also be members of other organizations that focus their attention on the Scottish Fold cat breed.

A reliable and trustworthy breeder, who is concerned about the welfare of their kittens, will not want to release them to new homes until they have received their initial vaccinations. This means that a good breeder will not sell their kittens until they are between the ages of 12 and 16 weeks of age.

By the age of 12 weeks, these kittens will already have been weaned, received their basic inoculations and will have started to become bonded with humans. An older kitten will also have the social and physical stability necessary for showing or being transported to their new home via airline service.

1. US Clubs, Registries & Breeders

When wondering where to begin your search for purchasing a Scottish Fold kitten in the United States, a good starting point will be to first check local clubs and registries.

Before choosing, please keep in mind that every cat is different - don't get this cat (or any cat, for that matter) because you had one before that was a sweetheart everybody loved. The reality of the situation is that the next Scottish Fold will more than likely be totally different.

American Cat Fanciers Association: *"...Founded by a group of cat fanciers in 1955, ACFA is known as the Fairest, Friendliest and most Fun feline association! Our goal is to promote the welfare, education, knowledge and interest in all domesticated, purebred and non-purebred cats, to breeders, owners, exhibitors of cats and the general public..."*

Cat Fanciers' Association, Inc.: *"...is a non-profit organization founded in 1906, that currently recognizes 42 pedigreed breeds for showing in the Championship Class. The Association licensed its first cat shows in 1906 and published the first Stud Book and Register in the Cat Journal..."*

The International Cat Association: *"...considered to be the world's largest genetic cat registry of pedigreed cats, household pet cats and kittens...TICA currently recognizes 71 breeds of cats for championship competition. TICA was the first and now the world's largest-registry to allow household cats of unknown ancestry to compete for the same titles and awards as pedigreed cats..."*

Wunderfolds Scottish Fold Cattery (in South Carolina): *"...Our cats are selected for their great looks and come from breed winning lines from across the world. All of our cats are raised in our home underfoot and kittens receive plenty of one-on-one attention and are well socialized and litter trained. Our kittens are health checked, wormed, vaccinated, microchipped and altered prior to being placed in their new homes. They are allowed to leave around 14 weeks of age..."*

Purrfect-Folds Cattery (in Arkansas): *"...Suzanne is a member of Cat Fanciers Association, has won awards at various CFA cat shows, is* on the Scottish Fold Breed Council and has qualified for the Cattery of Excellence Award from CFA. Our goal is to produce Scottish Folds that are not only unique and beautiful, but healthy and happy as well. All Scottish Fold kittens are raised with lots of love, attention and abundant human contact. They spend time in the veterinary clinic getting used to multiple people and animals - thus making the adjustment from our house to yours an easy transition. This means a happy and well-socialized Scottish Fold kitten for your new family member..."

2. UK Clubs, Registries & Breeders

When wondering where to begin your search for purchasing a Scottish Fold kitten in the United Kingdom, a good starting point will be to first check local clubs and registries.

Albafold (in Scotland): *"...Winter did us proud making 3 finals over the weekend. He was competing against some stunning kittens, we were thrilled with the wonderful comments from the Judges. Considering he was just 4 months old, we think our teddy bear did amazingly well. We are long forward to showing him this coming show season with TICA..."*

Lukaraza (in Kent): *"...All our kittens are grown in-house with other cats, two dogs and they are a part of our family. This ensures that they will have outgoing personalities, excellent temperaments and they will make fantastic companions in their new homes. We breed for quality but not for quantity...".*

3. Average Prices for Kittens

There can be a wide range of *"average"* pricing for any purebred cat, depending upon whether you want a show quality cat or simply a companion, with some adoptions or rescues beginning around $60 (£44). Keep in mind that the best age to purchase a kitten will be between 12 and 16 weeks.

Although you may find kittens for sale that cost less or more, or are free to good homes, there is a wide variety of prices from established breeders for this very popular purebred that may range between $850 and $1,800 (£639 and £1,354). Price will depend on the coat and eye color of the kittens, whether they are of show or companion quality, and the expertise and reputation of the particular breeder.

Important Note: the authors of this book have not purchased cats from breeders mentioned in this book, and we do not recommend any particular breeder.

Make sure that you thoroughly carry out your own research before purchasing a cat from any breeder. There are many cat breeders trading purely for profit and these often will not be overly concerned about the well-being of the cats they breed.

4. Avoiding Kitten Mills or Breeding Farms

As soon as a particular breed of cat becomes popular, they also become particularly susceptible to being bred by disreputable, high profit *"kitten mills"* or *"commercial breeding farms"*.

Kitten Mill breeding is especially prevalent with cute, smaller breeds or those with unusually colored or beautifully patterned coats, as it takes less space to mass-produce smaller pets.

This inhumane and cruel world of feline pregnancy for profit occurs all over the world, and if you are not very careful about where and how you purchase your kitten and are not concerned about purchasing your kitten from a reputable breeder, you may unknowingly end up promoting this disreputable practice.

Not only do Kitten Mills seriously contribute to overpopulation, they produce diseases and genetically flawed kittens that may suffer greatly with behavioral and/or health related problems that will cost their guardians greatly in terms of grief and stress and the unexpected financial burden associated with costly veterinarian intervention, while the kitten's life may be cut prematurely short.

These cats suffer in ways most of us could never imagine. For instance, most of these poor breeding cats have never walked on solid ground or felt grass, as they are housed in cramped wire cages. Females are bred continuously until they can no longer produce kittens, at which time they are killed or dumped on the side of a road.

It can be difficult to shut down these mills or mass-producing farming operations because, just like the drug trade, this is big business on a large and lucrative scale, and where there is money to be made exploiting innocent animals, these types of illicit operations will continue to exist.

Although Kitten Mill kittens are sold in a variety of different venues, pet stores are the main source for selling these unfortunate kittens, who are taken away from their mothers far too young (at 4 to 5 weeks of age) and sold to brokers, who pack them into crates to ship them off to pet stores. Many innocent kittens die during transportation.

While many pet stores are re-thinking their policy of keeping live pets for sale in their stores, until such time as everyone refuses to buy through a pet store, you will still see kittens and other smaller pets for sale in pet stores.

Think seriously before buying a kitten from a pet store, because almost all kittens found in pet stores (whether or not the employees working there are aware of it) are the result of inhumane kitten mill breeding. If you purchase one of these kittens, you are helping to enable and perpetuate this horribly cruel breeding practice.

Every time someone buys a kitten from a pet store, the store will order more from the Kitten Mill. As far as the pet store is concerned, the kittens are simply inventory, like treats or bags of cat food, and when one item drops off of the inventory list, another is purchased to replace it.

Kitten Mill kittens are also sold at flea markets, on the side of the road, at the beach, through newspaper ads and through fancy websites and Internet classifieds.

The only way to put these shameful, commercial businesses out of business is by spreading the word and never buying a kitten from a pet store, or any other advertising medium, unless you have first thoroughly checked them out by visiting the facility in person.

Always be wary if you answer an advertisement for a low-priced kitten for sale and the person selling then offers to deliver the kitten to you, because this could easily be the first sign that you are about to be involved in an illegal Kitten Mill operation.

Education is power, so educate yourself and spread the word to others about Kitten Mills, because this is the first step toward ensuring that yourself and everyone you know are never unknowingly involved in the suffering that is forced upon the breeding cats and kittens trapped in a kitten mill or mass-farming operation.

5. How to Choose the Right Kitten

Choosing the <u>right</u> kitten for your family and your lifestyle is more important than you might imagine. Many people do not give serious enough thought to sharing their home with a new kitten before they actually bring one home.

Don't let this be a spontaneous decision and don't choose a kitten based solely on what it looks like, because the breed may currently be popular, because you saw one in a TV movie, or because your best friend has one or your family had the same kind of cat when they were growing up. None of these are good reasons for sharing your life with a cat.

a) Important Questions: in order to be fair to ourselves, our family and the kitten or cat we choose to share our lives with, we humans need to take a serious look at our life, both as it is today and what we envision it being in twelve to fifteen years, and then ask ourselves a few important, personal questions, and honestly answer them before making the commitment to a kitten, such as:

- Do I have the time and patience necessary to devote to a kitten, which will grow into a cat that needs me to feed and care for it?

- Have I done my research about the breed I'm interested in, so that I can properly raise and socialize a kitten?

- Do I spend the majority of my working or leisure time away from the home, or do I work at home and spend my leisure time around the home?

- Do I like to travel a lot? Leaving an animal that relies on you for food, shelter and companionship alone all the time just isn't fair.

- Am I a neat freak or do I have allergies? Almost all cats constantly shed their hair and it will be all over the home and your clothes, and you could be allergic to the cat's dander.

- Do I have a young, growing family that takes up all my spare time and are my children old enough to carefully handle a kitten? Very young children tend not to be especially gentle with small pets and the kitten may react badly by biting or scratching.

- Can I afford the food costs and the veterinarian expenses that are part of being a responsible and conscientious cat guardian?

- Is the decision to bring a kitten into my life a family decision, or just for the children, who often quickly lose interest?

- Have I thoroughly researched the breed I'm interested in, and is it truly compatible with my lifestyle or am I considering this breed because I had a similar cat when I was a child, or just because I like the way it looks?

- What is the number one reason why I want a cat in my life?

Once you ask yourself these important questions and honestly answer them, you will have a much better understanding of the type of kitten or cat that would be best suited for you and your family.

If you are too busy for a cat or choose the wrong cat that is not compatible with you or your family's energy and lifestyle, you will inevitably end up with an unhappy cat, which will lead to behavioral issues, which then will lead to an unhappy family and worse, another cat being abandoned at the local SPCA or rescue.

Please take the time to choose wisely. If you have absolutely decided that the Scottish Fold is the right cat for you, the following tips will help you to choose the right kitten from the litter.

b) Careful Kitten Selection: although your breeder can often help you with selecting the right kitten for you and your family, after observing the kittens playing, you will likely be feeling especially drawn to one kitten over another.

Beyond your feelings for any particular kitten in the litter, carefully considering other factors will help to improve the odds of you having a positive guardianship experience with your new kitten.

For instance, take your emotions out of the picture for a moment and instead be a little objective when evaluating each kitten in the litter, because doing so can help you to make the right choice.

While some people may become overly emotional when choosing a kitten, and can be especially attracted to those who display extremes in behavior because they want to *"save"* them, it's not a particularly good idea to choose a kitten that may be very shy or frightened in the hope that they may grow into a happy, well-adjusted cat.

Some people will delve even further into their emotional desires or needs to *"save"* or *"rescue"*.

Even though you may be one of those humans who has a strong desire to "rescue" those appearing to be less fortunate, when it comes time to choose a healthy kitten, it's simply not the best idea to choose a particular kitten because it may seem weaker than the rest of the kittens or has obvious health or behavioral issues, because you want to provide it with a chance that you believe the kitten might not otherwise have.

While it is certainly wonderful that we humans have the capacity to raise and care for kittens that may be afflicted with health or behavior problems, it's important that these types of decisions are not undertaken lightly, as such challenges can lead you down a path that could be an emotional roller coaster of highs and lows that can cause problems for both feline and human alike and that could also involve very substantial veterinarian costs.

While many minor behavioral problems can be modified with early training, it's important to be aware that the time and effort needed to do so will be difficult to predict and you should be aware that *"rescuing"* a cat that could grow up to have behavioral problems may require more than you are capable of providing in the long run.

c) Pick of the Litter: generally speaking, when choosing a kitten out of a litter, look for one that is friendly and outgoing, rather than one who is overly aggressive or fearful.

Taking note of a kitten's social skills when they are still with their litter mates will help you to choose the right kitten to take home, because kittens who demonstrate good social skills with their litter mates are much more likely to develop into easy going, happy adults who play well with others and will more easily integrate into their new forever homes.

In a social setting where all the kittens can be observed together, there are several important observations you can make, including:

(1) When the kittens are playing, notice which kittens are comfortable both on top and on the bottom when play fighting and wresting with their littermates, and which kittens seem to only like being on top.
Kittens who don't mind being on the bottom or who appear to be fine with either position will usually play well with others when they become adults.

(2) If the kittens have toys to play with, observe which kittens try to keep the toys away from the other kittens and which kittens share.
Those who want to hoard the toys and keep all other kittens away may be more aggressive with other cats over food or treats, or in play where toys are involved as they become older.

(3) Notice which kittens seem to like the company of the other kittens and which ones seem to be loners. Kittens who like the company of their littermates are more likely to be interested in the company of other cats and pets, such as the family dog, as they mature, than anti-social kittens that prefer their own solitude.

(4) Observe the reaction of kittens that meow or spit when they bite or roughhouse with another kitten too roughly. Kittens who ease up when another kitten cries or spits are more likely to respond appropriately when they play too roughly as adults.

(5) In addition, check to see if the kitten you are interested in is sociable with people, because if they will not come to you or display hissing or fear of humans, this may be a problem when they become adults.

(6) Furthermore, always check if the kitten you are interested in is relaxed and interested in you when you pick them up and will allow you to hold them for a couple of minutes without fighting to get away.

6. How to Check If a Kitten is Healthy

Of course, you will want to check if a kitten you are considering taking home is not just emotionally healthy, but also physically healthy.

First, ask to see veterinarian reports from the breeder as first shots are due anywhere between 6 and 8 weeks, to satisfy yourself that the kitten is as healthy as possible, and then once you make your decision to share your life with a particular kitten, make an appointment with your own veterinarian for a complete examination.

Before you get to this stage, however, there are a few general signs of good health to be aware of when choosing a healthy kitten from a litter, including the following:

- Breathing – a healthy kitten will breathe quietly, without coughing or sneezing, and there will be no crusting or discharge around their nostrils

- Body – they will look round and well fed, with an obvious layer of fat over their rib cage

- Coat – a healthy kitten will have a soft coat with no dandruff, dullness, greasiness or bald spots

- Energy – a well-rested kitten will be alert and energetic

- Genitals – a healthy kitten will not have any sort of discharge visible in or around their genital or anal regions

- Hearing – a healthy kitten with good hearing should react if you clap your hands behind their head

- Mobility – a healthy kitten will walk and run normally without wobbling, limping or seeming to be weak, stiff or sore

- Vision – a healthy kitten will have bright, clear eyes without crust or discharge and they should notice if an enticing string or feather is drawn past them within their field of vision

7. One Scottish Fold Cat or Two?

While getting two kittens at once will be twice the fun, it will also be twice the work, which means that you will need to be doubly alert and patient, and perhaps also lose even more sleep than you bargained for during the kitten phase.

Every kitten needs your constant attention and guidance, therefore, before taking the plunge, ask yourself if you have the time and energy to provide constant attention and guidance for two little kittens that could be running in opposite directions?

Many humans decide to get two kittens, because they want their kitten to have someone to play with and for company during times when they cannot be at home.

Be careful that one of the reasons for this decision is not based on the fact that the human making this decision might not be the ideal candidate for having one kitten, let alone two.

For instance, if the reason you are considering two kittens is so that the one kitten will not be alone all day while you are at work, stop right there, because leaving one, two or a dozen kittens alone all day while you are at work may be a terrible decision.

Another consideration when thinking about whether or not to get two kittens is that often when they grow up, there may be continual sibling rivalry as each kitten vies for your attention.

Something you may not have considered, is that it is entirely possible that when the kittens mature, they will no longer get along with each other as well as they once did when they were young kittens, especially if both are the same sex.

Furthermore, when you have two kittens growing up together, one will always be the more dominant personality that will take over the other, and this could mean that neither kitten will fully develop their individual personalities.

As well, when you have two kittens or cats in your life, they generally tend to be less affectionate or interested in their human guardians as they have each other to rely upon. This can mean that they will focus so much on each other that they may bond much less with you.

Each kitten will require our individual attention when it comes time for teaching house rules, and having two kittens in the picture can make it very difficult for them to concentrate or focus on the job at hand.

8. The Best Age to Purchase a Kitten

Generally speaking, no kitten (including a Scottish Fold kitten) should be removed from their mother any earlier than 8 weeks of age and leaving them until they are 10 to 16 weeks of age may be preferred, because this will give them the extra time they need to learn important life skills from the mother cat, including eating solid food and grooming.

In the case of the Scottish Fold breed, responsible breeders will often not release their kittens to their new homes until they are between the ages of 14 and 16 weeks; at this time they will have been weaned, received their basic inoculations and will have started to become bonded with humans.

In addition, leaving a kitten amongst their littermates for a longer period of time will help to ensure that they learn socialization skills. Removing a kitten from the mother and other siblings too early could mean that they will miss out on valuable skills and may not socialize well with others.

For the first month of a kitten's life they will be on a mother's milk only diet. Once the kitten's teeth begin to appear, they will start to be weaned from mother's milk and by the age of 8 weeks should be completely weaned and eating just kitten food.

Removing a kitten from their mother any earlier than eight weeks could mean they are not fully weaned and they would be much more difficult to feed.

9. Should I Get a Male or Female Cat?

Everyone you ask will have a personal opinion about whether you should get a male or a female of any breed.

While you will find just as many humans preferring a male cat over a female, and often our preferences or results of opinion polls are just what we are used to, if you are a first-time cat guardian there may be a few considerations that can help you to make a more informed decision.

For instance, a poll carried out a few years ago reported that, *"...55% of respondents thought that male cats made for better, more affectionate pets, while 25% came out in favor of female cats, and 19% believed that the cat's sex was irrelevant..."*

While some people clearly harbor strong feelings on the subject, with some humans believing that female cats are bossier and more independent, and male cats are cuddlier or more laid back. Having had both male and female cats myself, it is my experience that male and female cats each equally possess the same characteristics.

As an example, I once had a male cat that was very "female" in nature as he mothered the younger cats and kittens that became part of my family.

Something more practical to take into consideration when choosing a male over a female cat is that when spaying and neutering your cat, the operation is much more invasive when spaying a female, than the simpler neutering process required for males.

Interesting is that some humans pick their cats based on sex alone, because they cannot stop themselves from attributing human characteristics to their chosen cats, and therefore attribute male and female characteristics to their cats based on their human experience of men and women.

This is (of course) complete nonsense, because a cat is a cat, and it can be harmful to your relationship to project human emotions onto them or imagine that they will act like humans just because we are human.

Therefore, the best way to choose your kitten will be to take your time observing the litter when you visit the breeder.

10. The Scottish Fold Cat Shopping List

Before bringing home your new kitten or cat for the first time, there will be a list of items you need to make sure you have on hand, including:

Food – usually the kitten will remain on whatever food they have been fed at the breeder's for at least the first couple of weeks, until they are well settled in their new home, so make sure you ask the breeder what brand to buy. Typical yearly food costs might be anywhere from $80 to $200 (£59 and £148) or more.

Food and Water Bowls – make sure they are small enough for a young kitten to get close to, so that they can easily eat and drink. Depending upon whether you choose a simple stainless bowl set or want to provide your cat with automatic feeders, what you choose for your cat can range from $5 to $200 (£4 to £148).

Kennel – when you buy your kitten's hard-sided kennel, make sure that you buy the size that will be appropriate for them when they are fully grown. It must be large enough so that (when fully grown) they can easily stand up and turn around inside it. You may expect to pay between $20 and $80 (£15 and £59) for a solid carrier.

Litter Box – there are many types of boxes to choose from including the standard open box, the completely closed box, the hooded box, and the self-cleaning litter box, as well as the box to help your cat transition to using the toilet. The typical cost may range between $10 and $200 (£7 and £148), and whichever you choose for your cat, you may have to start off with a small one, or one with a ramp that your small kitten can get into.

Climbing Tree, Tower or Condo – there are a wide variety of climbing trees, towers and condos on the market, some with just open perches and some with completely enclosed small spaces where your cat can hide or snooze in seclusion, or a combination of both, and some can even satisfy your cat's need to scratch.

You will have to decide on how much space you have and where to establish this kitty *"furniture"*, so that it can safely fit into your home, and you can expect to pay anywhere between $70 and $150 (£52 and £111) with some of the more exotic and elaborate condos being considerably more costly (upwards of $2,000 (£1,477).

Scratching Post – there are also many different types of "scratchers" and what you decide to purchase for your cat will depend on the space you have, because they can be tall and thin poles, triangular or square shaped and you can even get your cat a door hanger scratcher. Expect to pay between $20 and $100 (£15 and £74) to keep your cat's nails nicely sharpened.

Leash and Harness – if you intend to walk your cat on a leash, you'd better begin this process when they are kittens, or you will have a squirming, angry cat on your hands. The Scottish Fold is particularly easy to train and may enjoy learning tricks.

You will need to buy new harnesses as your kitten grows in size and as far as the leash is concerned, get one that is made from lightweight nylon with a small clip on the end and no more than 6-8 feet (183 to 244 cm) in length, because too long will mean your cat can get tangled around bushes and other hazards. Cost for a secure leash and harness will be approximately $10 to $35 (£7 to £26).

Soft Beds – while your kitten or cat may or may not prefer sleeping in the nice comfy beds you bought for them, you can train and encourage them to use their beds, so make sure that you purchase one or two for comfortable sleeping when they are not sleeping in your shoes, on top of the fridge or inside a paper bag or box. Comfortable beds may range in price between $20 and $100 (£15 and £74).

Make sure that you buy the beds large enough for a full-grown cat or get larger ones as your cat grows in size.

Feline Shampoo and Conditioner – sometimes even a cat needs a bath. Always choose products that are the correct pH for a cat (never use human products). You will also need a non-slip mat for the sink or bathtub and lots of drying towels.

The price of shampoo and conditioner can vary considerably, depending on whether it is natural and organic and the brand chosen. Generally speaking, you can expect to pay anywhere between $15 and $40 (£11 and £30) for shampoo and $25 to $65 (£18 to £48) for a good conditioner.

Finger Tooth Brush –- this is a soft, rubber cap that fits over the human's finger (typical cost: $4 - $8 or £3 - £6) to get the kitten used to having their teeth regularly brushed. Later on, consider transitioning to a regular toothbrush (typical cost: $16 - $28 or £12 - £21) or an electric toothbrush for superior cleaning (an Oral-B electric is best) for a cost of approximately $30 (£22).

Soft Bristle Brush or Comb for longer coats – for daily grooming, for a cost of $10 to $15 (£7 to £11).

Kitten Nail Scissors – for trimming their toenails – just snip off the curve at the end of the nail. Most pet stores carry these scissors and you can expect to pay anywhere between $6 and $15 (£4 and £11).

Interactive Toys – most cats love an interactive toy (one that moves) or a "fishing pole" type of toy that is a pole with an invisible line, with a feather or piece of leather tied at the end. These types of toys will provide endless hours of fun for both kitten or cat and human, and may range in price between $10 and $30 (£7 and £22) or more.

Daily Essentials – Beyond choosing the best food for your kitten or cat, you will also want to choose healthy treats and litter than is non-toxic and kind to the environment.

Treats can range in price between $8 and $20 (£6 and £15) or more.

Cat Litter can also vary quite a bit in price and may cost between $10 and $35 (£7 and £26) for a bag.

Be sure to take your shopping list with you when you go to your local pet store or boutique, otherwise you may forget critical items.

NOTE: if you do not already have a hairdryer, you will need to get one of these too, so you can dry your kitten or cat after bath time.

Chapter 8: Kitten Proofing Your Home

Most kittens will be a curious bundle of energy, eager to explore everything, which means that they will get into everything within their reach and can easily disappear from sight.

As a responsible kitten guardian, you will want to provide a safe environment for them, which means eliminating all sources of danger, similar to what you would do for a curious toddler.

Be aware that your kitten will want to touch, sniff, taste, chew, investigate and closely inspect every electrical cord, every closet, every nook and cranny of your home and everything you may have left lying about on the floor.

Power cords can be found in just about every room in the home and to a teething kitten, these may look like irresistible, fun chew toys. Make sure that you tuck all power cords securely out of your kitten's reach or enclose them inside a chew-proof PVC tube.

Kitchen – first of all, there are many human foods that can be harmful to cats (see Chapter 18), therefore, your kitchen should always be strictly off limits to your kitten any time you are preparing food. Calmly send them out of the kitchen any time you are in the kitchen, and they will quickly get the idea that this area is off limits to them.

Bathroom – bathroom cupboards and drawers or the side of a bathtub where you may leave your shaving supplies can hold many dangers for a young and curious kitten.

Kleenex, cotton swabs, Q-tips, toilet paper, razors, pills, soap or other materials left within your kitten's reach are an easy target that could result in an emergency visit to your veterinarian's office.

Family members need to learn to put shampoos, soap, facial products, makeup and accessories out of reach or safely inside a cabinet or drawer.

Bedroom – if you don't keep your shoes, slippers and clothing safely behind doors, you may find that your kitten has claimed them for their new bathroom.

Be vigilant about keeping everything in its safe place, including jewellery, hair ties, bills, coins, and other items small enough for them to swallow in containers or drawers, and secure any exposed cords or wires.

If you have children, make sure they understand that, especially while your kitten is going through their exploratory stage, they must keep their rooms picked up and leave nothing that could cause a choking problem to the kitten lying about on the floor or within their reach.

Living Room – we humans spend many hours in our cosy gathering places to watch movies or play games, and often the living areas of our homes will have many items that are very enticing for a curious kitten.

You will want to keep your home free of excess clutter and remain vigilant about straightening up and putting things out of sight that could be tempting to your kitten.

Office – we often spend a great deal of time in our home offices, which means that our kitten will want to be there, too, and they will be curious about all the items an office has to offer, such as pens, pencils, paperclips, staples, elastic bands, and electrical cords.

Although your kitten might think that rubber bands or paper clips are fun to play with, allowing these items to be within your kitten's reach could end up being a fatal mistake if your kitten swallows them.

Plants – can be a very tempting target for your kitten's teeth, so you will want to keep them well out their reach. If you have floor plants, they will need to be moved to a shelf or counter or placed behind a closed door until your curious fur friend grows out of the habit of putting everything in their mouth. Also, keep in mind that many common houseplants are poisonous to cats (discussed in Chapter 18).

Garage and Yard – there are obvious, as well as subtle, dangers that could seriously harm or even kill a kitten, which can often be found in the garage or yard.

Some of these might include antifreeze, gasoline, fertilizers, rat, mice, snail and slug poison, weed killer, paint, cleaners and solvents, grass seed, bark mulch and various insecticides.

If you are storing any of these toxic substances in your garage or garden shed, make certain that you keep all such products inside a locked cabinet, or stored on high shelves that your kitten will not be able to reach.

Even better, choose not to use toxic chemicals anywhere in your home or garden.

1. Kitten Hazard Home Inspection

Every conscientious kitten guardian needs to take a serious look around the home not just from the human eye level, but also from the eye level of a Scottish Fold kitten.

This means literally crawling around your floors, which can be a fun exercise to ask your children to help you with.

Your kitten has a much lower vantage point than you do when standing, therefore, there may be items in your environment that could potentially be harmful to a kitten that a human might not notice unless you get down on the floor and take a really good look.

Remember that many cats are food motivated, and enticed by small objects they find on the floor, therefore they will put everything into their mouth and it will be up to you to ensure that they do not eat something that could harm them.

2. The First Weeks With Your Kitten

a) The First Night: before you go to the breeder's to pick up your new kitten, vacuum your floors, including all the dust bunnies under the bed.

Do a last-minute check of every room to make sure that everything that could be a kitten hazard is carefully tucked away out of sight and that nothing is left on the floor or low down on shelves where a curious kitten might get into trouble.

Close most of the doors inside your home, so that there are just one or two rooms that the kitten will have access to. You have already been shopping and have everything you need, so take out the litter box and have it ready when you bring your new furry friend home.

Also have your soft bed(s) in an area where you will be spending most of your time and where your kitten can easily find them. If you have already purchased a soft toy, take the toy with you when you go to pick up your kitten.

NOTE: take either your hard-sided kennel or your soft-sided "Sherpa" travel bag (lined with pee pads) with you when going to bring your new kitten home, and make sure that it is securely fastened to the seat of your vehicle with the seatbelt restraint system.

Even though you will be tempted to hold your new kitten in your lap on the drive home, this is a very dangerous place for them to be, in case of an accident. Place them inside their kennel or bag, which will be lined with soft towels and perhaps even a warm, towel-wrapped hot water bottle (and a pee pad) and close the door.

If you have a friend who can drive for you, sit beside your kitten in the back seat, and if they cry on the way home, remind them that they are not alone with your soft, soothing voice.

Before bringing your new kitten inside your home, if there is a place in your garden where you want them to relieve themselves (if they will be an outdoor cat), first take them there (or to their litter box) and try to wait it out long enough for them to at least go pee.

Then bring them inside your home and introduce them to where their food and water bowls will be kept in case they are hungry or thirsty.

Let your kitten wander around sniffing and checking out their new surroundings and encourage them to follow you wherever you go. Show them where the litter box is located, which you have placed in a room (maybe the bathroom) where it is quiet and where they can easily find it.

If you plan to have your cat travel with you, now is the time to get them used to sleeping inside their hard-sided kennel, so find a corner in your bedroom and put them inside with the door open, while you sit on the floor in front of it and quietly encourage them to relax inside their kennel.

Depending on the time of day you bring your new kitten home for the first time, practice this kennel exercise several times throughout the day, and if they will take a little treat each time you encourage them to go inside their kennel, this will help to further encourage the behavior of them wanting to go inside.

After they have had their evening meal, take them outside or to their litter box approximately 5 – 10 minutes later to go to the bathroom, and when they do, make sure you praise them and perhaps even give a little treat.

So far your kitten has only been allowed in several rooms of your home, as you have kept the other doors closed, so keep it this way for the first few days.

Before it's time for bed, again take your kitten to their litter box, or outside to the garden where they last went potty (if they will be an outdoor cat) and make sure that they go pee before bringing them back inside.

Before bed, prepare your kitten's hot water bottle and wrap it in a towel so that it will not be too hot for them, and place it inside their hard-sided kennel (in your bedroom).

Turn the lights down low and invite your kitten to go inside their kennel and if they seem interested, perhaps give them a soft toy to have inside with them.

Let them walk into the kennel under their own steam and when they do, give them a little treat (if they are interested) and encourage them to snuggle down to sleep while you are sitting on the floor in front of the kennel. Remember that they have been used to sleeping all curled up with their warm siblings and their mother.

Once they have settled down inside their kennel, close the door, go to your bed and turn all the lights off. It may help your kitten to sleep during their first night home if you can play quiet, soothing music in the background.

If they start to cry, stay calm and have compassion because this is the first time in their young life when they do not have the comfort of their mother or their littermates.

Do not let them out of their kennel if they are crying, but rather, simply reassure them with your calm voice that they are not alone until they fall asleep and if your bed is wide enough to accommodate your kitten's kennel, and they seem to relax when closer to you, it may help them to fall asleep for the first few nights in their new kennel if you have it beside you on top of the bed, so that you are closer to them.

If there is any danger of the kennel falling off the bed during the night, do NOT do this, as you will traumatize your kitten and make them afraid of their kennel.

b) The First Week: during the first week, you and your new kitten will be getting settled into their new routine, which will involve you getting used to your kitten's needs as they also get used to your usual schedule.

Be as consistent as possible with your waking and sleeping routine, getting up and going to bed at the same time each day, so that it will be easier for your kitten to get into the flow and routine of their new life. If you have blackout curtains on your bedroom window, it will be easier for your kitten to sleep longer.

First thing in the morning, remove your kitten from their kennel and take them immediately to their litter box, or outside to relieve himself or herself at the place where they last went pee.

At this time, if you are teaching them to ring a doorbell to go outside, let them ring the bell before you go out the door with them, whether you are carrying them, or whether they are walking out the door on their own.

NOTE: during the first week, you may want to carry your kitten to his or her litter box, or outside first thing in the morning, as they may not be able to hold it for very long once waking up. Now is the time to begin leash and harness training.

When you bring them back inside, you can let them follow you so they get used to their new leash and/or harness arrangement. Be very careful not to drag your kitten if they stop or pull back on the leash.

If they refuse to walk on the leash, just hold the tension toward you (without pulling) while encouraging them to walk toward you, until they start to move forward again.

Now it will be time for their first feed of the day, and after they have finished eating, keep an eye on the clock, because you will want to take them to their litter box or outside to relieve themselves in about 5 – 10 minutes.

When your kitten is not eating or napping, they will be wanting to explore and have little play sessions, where they are hunting imaginary prey and these times will help you bond with your kitten more and more each day.

As their new guardian, it will be your responsibility to keep a close eye on them throughout the day, so that you can notice when they need to relieve themselves and either take them to their litter box or take them outside.

You will also need to make sure that they are eating and drinking enough throughout the day, so set regular feeding times at least three times a day.

If you plan to leash train your kitten, also set specific times in the day when you will take your kitten out for a little walk on leash and harness, so that they are not only going outside when they need to relieve themselves, but they are also learning to explore their new neighbourhood with you beside them.

When your kitten is still very young, you will not want to walk for a long time as they will get tired easily, and you do not want to stress joints or bones that are growing, so keep your walks to no more than 5 or 10 minutes during your first week and if they seem tired or cold, pick them up and carry them home.

3. Common Mistakes to Avoid

1) Sleeping in Your Bed: many people make the mistake of allowing a crying kitten to sleep with them in their bed, and while this may help to calm and comfort a new kitten, it will set a dangerous precedent because a sleeping human body can easily crush a small kitten.

As much as it may pull on your heart strings to hear your new kitten crying the first couple of nights in their kennel, a little tough love at the beginning will keep them safe in their kennel while teaching them that this is their safe sanctuary.

2) Picking Them Up at the Wrong Time: never pick your kitten up if they display nervousness, fear or aggression (such as growling) toward an object, person or other pet (unless they are in danger of being attacked), because this will be rewarding them for unbalanced behaviour.

Instead, your kitten needs to be gently corrected by you, with firm and calm energy so that they learn not to react with fear or aggression.

3) Armpit Alligators: when your cat is a small size, be aware that many guardians get into the bad habit of carrying a small cat or kitten far too much. They need to be on the ground and walking on their own so that they do not become overly confident because a cat that is carried by their guardian is literally being placed in the *"top cat"* position.

Humans who constantly carry small cats around, rather than allowing them to walk on their own, can often inadvertently create what I refer to as an *"armpit alligator"* situation.

This happens when the cat becomes possessive of its guardian who carries it everywhere, and when another adult or child sees the cute little cat and approaches to say hello, the cute little cat who has been inadvertently trained to believe that it is the boss may then hiss, growl or scratch.

4) Playing Too Hard or Too Long: many humans play too hard or allow their children to play too long or too roughly with a young kitten. You need to remember that a young kitten tires very easily and especially during the critical growing phases of their young life, they need their rest.

5) Hand Play: always discourage your kitten from chewing or biting your hands, or any part of your body for that matter.

If you allow them to do this when they are kittens, they will want to continue to do so when they have strong jaws and adult teeth and this is not acceptable behavior for any breed of cat.

Do not get into the habit of playing the *"hand"* game, where you rough up the kitten and slide them across the floor with your hands, because this will teach your kitten that your hands are playthings and you will have to work hard to break this bad habit.

When your kitten is teething, they will naturally want to chew on everything within reach, and this will include you. As cute as you might think it is, this is not an acceptable behavior and you need to gently, but firmly, discourage the habit.

A light flick with a finger on the end of a kitten nose, combined with a firm *"NO"* and removing the enticing fingers by making a fist when they are trying to attack or bite human fingers will discourage them from this activity.

6) Not Getting Used to Grooming: not taking the time to get your kitten used to a regular grooming routine, including bathing, brushing, toenail clipping and teeth brushing can lead to a lifetime of trauma for both human and cat every time these procedures must be performed.

It will be important for the health of your cat to set aside a few minutes each day for your grooming routine.

NOTE: get your cat used to being up high, on a table or countertop when you are grooming them, because when it comes time for a full grooming session, or a visit to the vet's office where they will be placed on an examination table, then they will not be stressed by being placed in an unfamiliar situation.

7) Free Feeding: means to keep food in your kitten's bowl 24/7 so that they can eat any time of the day or night, whenever they feel like it.

While free feeding a young kitten can be a good idea (especially with very small cats) until they are about four or five months old, many guardians often get into the bad habit of allowing their adult cats to continue to eat food any time they want (free feeding), by leaving food out 24/7.

Getting into this type of habit can be a serious mistake, as you need to be in control of their food, so that they do not become picky eaters or eat too much and become unhealthily overweight, which can lead to many health problems later in life.

8) Treating Them Like Children: do not get into the bad habit of treating your cat like a small, furry human, because even though they may put up with wearing hats and being dressed in doll's clothing, they don't really like it, and not honoring them for the amazing cat they are will only cause them confusion that could lead to behavioural problems.

IMPORTANT: remember that the one thing your Scottish Fold is the absolute best at is being a cat.

A well-balanced cat needs to understand the house rules and boundaries, so that they can live a contented, happy and stress-free life.

9) Distraction and Replacement: when your kitten tries to chew on your hand, foot, clothing or anything else that is not fair game, you need to firmly and calmly tell them "*No*", and then distract them by replacing what they are not supposed to be chewing with a toy.

Make sure that you happily praise them every time they choose the toy to chew on. If the kitten persists in chewing on you, remove yourself from the equation by getting up and walking away.

If they are really persistent, put them inside their kennel with a favorite toy until they calm down.

Always praise your kitten when they stop inappropriate behavior or replace inappropriate behavior with something that is acceptable to you, so that they begin to understand what they can and cannot do.

4. Bonding With Your Cat

You will begin bonding with your kitten or cat from the very first moment you bring him or her home from the breeder.

This is the time when your kitten or cat will be the most upset and nervous, as they will no longer have the guidance, warmth and comfort of their mother or their other littermates, and you will need to take on the role of being your new fur friend's centre of attention.

Be patient, kind and gentle with them as they are learning that you are now their new centre of the universe.

Your daily interaction with your kitten during play sessions and especially your disciplined exercises, including going for walks on a leash (if you choose to leash train them), and teaching commands and tricks, will all be wonderful bonding opportunities.

Depending on the particular personality of each cat, the Scottish Fold may be a cat that likes to sit on your lap, or they may prefer to sit beside you, or somewhere near you and may follow you from room to room.

Do not make the mistake of thinking that *"bonding"* with your new kitten can only happen if you are playing together, because the very best bonding happens when you are establishing a feeding and bathroom routine and kindly teaching house rules.

Chapter 9: Meowing and Tail Twitching

1. What Does the Meow Mean?

Of course, our cats meow for a wide variety of reasons, and every cat is different, depending upon their natural breed tendencies (Siamese tend to be more vocal) and how they were raised, and this section discusses some of the more common reasons why a cat might be meowing.

Apparently, scientists have identified more than a dozen different cat meows, that each have their own meaning, beginning with kittens that meow to communicate with their mother and hissing, growling, squealing, howling and screaming to talk with each other.

Interestingly, adult cats meow solely to communicate with us humans and as you learn your cat's language and become more attuned to their different meows, you will be able to tell the differences between "boredom", "hungry", "hurt" or "scared" meows.

a) Communication: since the very first wild cat, they have communicated over long distances by howling to one another and when in closer proximity, growling, hissing or snarling to warn off other cats approaching what they consider to be their territory.

Now, our domesticated cats have learned to vocalize for a wide variety of reasons, such as meowing upon greeting or in anticipation of their favorite food, growling when they are afraid or frustrated, or purring when they are happy and content.

b) Danger: many feline companions will alert us to unusual circumstances by acting agitated, jumping up or meowing, and we need to learn identify this behavior and pay attention.

We want our cats to tell us when there is real imminent danger and in this case, should the danger involve an unwanted intruder, we want them to "tell" us something is not right.

For instance, years ago I lived in a basement apartment with my cat, Charlie. I was just getting out of the shower when Charlie kept meowing, acting agitated, and jumping up on the window sill for no apparent reason. Then I noticed movement outside my window and saw a peeping tom (not a cat) trying to peer through the window. I immediately called 911 and the police arrived to apprehend the offending person. Big thanks to my cat, Charlie, for alerting me to this potentially dangerous situation.

When our cats are acting strange for a reason we are not yet aware of, we need to pay attention and calmly assess the situation rather than immediately becoming annoyed.

We also need to remember that our cat's sense of smell, hearing and sometimes eyesight is far more acute than our own, so we need to give them an opportunity to tell us they just heard, saw or sensed something that they are worried or uncertain about.

We should not be ignoring our cats (or yelling at them) when they are attempting to "tell" us that something is bothering them, even if we ourselves understand that the noise the cat just heard is only the gardener getting ready to water the flowerbed.

We need to calmly acknowledge the cat's concern by saying, *"OK, "good boy"* or *" good girl"* and then asking them to come to you. This way you have quietly and calmly let your cat know that the situation is nothing to be concerned about and you have asked them to move away from the target they are concerned about, which will usually put a stop to the agitated behavior.

c) Attention: many cats will get up to all sorts of antics to get their owner's attention, just because they are bored or want a treat or to be let out in the back yard.

For instance, you may come home to find that the entire roll of toilet paper is now on the bathroom floor or dragged all through the house or your Christmas tree has been a climbing post and is now lying flat on the floor.

Also, remember to stay calm when a cat is demanding attention because even negative attention can be rewarding for a cat that can then learn further habits that could become a daily annoyance for the human side of the relationship.

d) Boredom: many cats, especially those who have not been properly socialized or that have not been allowed to understand that they have rules and boundaries, may get up to all sorts of mischievous behavior when left at home alone and they are bored or are feeling the anxiety of being alone.

e) Fear or Pain: cats are not usually very good at letting you know when they are in pain, unless it is very severe, at which time they may moan or cry.

Learn to notice your cat's usual behavior, so that when they are acting out of the ordinary, you will notice and you can quickly respond and offer the assistance that they may need.

Whatever reason your cat may be meowing, always remember that this is how they communicate and "tell" us that they want something or are concerned, afraid, nervous or unhappy about something, and as their guardians, we humans need to pay attention.

2. What Does the Tail Tell You?

There are many emotions conveyed through the cat's tail from friendship to aggression and you might want to become familiar with some of these tail subtleties, so that you can more easily understand your cat's mood or emotional state.

For instance, a tail that is held straight up usually means that the cat is feeling content and friendly, while a tail carried straight up, but with a hook at the end can mean the cat is friendly, but unsure.

Also, a cat with a tail held straight up, but quivering can mean they are very happy to see you, or they may be about to spray your favorite couch.

A cat that is in a potentially aggressive mood may carry their tail straight and in the down position, and as they become more agitated and defensive, the tail position may switch to one side or the other, or when in a sitting position the tail may thrash from side to side. A dramatically swishing tail usually means that something has upset the cat and he or she wants to be left alone.

A twitching tail in a seated cat can mean they are alert and interested in something that has caught their attention, whereas a tail carried down and between the legs will mean that your cat is feeling nervous and submissive.

The Halloween tail is what I like to refer to as that fully bristled, straight up tail that looks very much like a bottle brush, and that can mean the cat is very angry or simply that they just received a shocking fright.

Sometimes a cat will entwine their tail with another cat's tail or around your legs or other objects and this is their way of marking their territory or trying to manipulate or get our attention, perhaps so we will feed them.

As well, the speed the tail is moving at will also give you an idea of the mental state of the cat because the speed of the wag usually indicates how annoyed a cat may be.

While certainly a cat's tail can help us humans to understand how our cats might be feeling, there are many other factors to take into consideration when determining a cat's state of mind.

Chapter 10: Scottish Fold Cat Health Concerns

How healthy your cat may be is very much up to you and how informed you are about food, environmental issues and general care of your feline friend.

Healthy Teeth = Healthy Cat

We humans brush our teeth everyday, but how many pet lovers actually do the same for their fur friends? Just the same as good dental hygiene helps to keep us humans healthy, the same is true for our dogs and cats.

Imagine what your teeth would feel like and what your breath might smell like if you never brushed your teeth and then get started caring for your cat's teeth because doing so will play a very important role in your cat's overall health and wellbeing.

Consider that while neglected teeth cause bad breath, plaque and bacterial build up in your cat's mouth, the problem doesn't stop there because this type of neglect will eventually lead to periodontal dental disease and the bacterial infection will spread throughout the cat's body to cause eventual organ damage that can result in heart, kidney and lung problems.

While brushing your cat's teeth may not be yours or your cat's favorite thing to do, daily brushing will ensure that your cat's mouth stays as disease-free as possible and the best time to start daily brushing is as soon as your kitten has permanent teeth, at around 6 months of age.

You can start brushing with a finger brush or a small, soft bristle brush and feline toothpaste (do NOT use human toothpaste), before the adult teeth to get them used to the process, and once they are used to the procedure, you might want to slowly graduate them to getting used to an electric toothbrush, which will do a superior job of cleaning the teeth and removing plaque from the gum line.

Of course, if you bring an adult cat into your home, getting him or her used to the daily teeth brushing ritual may take much time and determination will be needed to get them acclimated to the procedure.

Do not underestimate the importance of keeping your cat's teeth in good shape, because doing so will have a direct link to improving their health and quality of life and helping them to live longer, so make sure that you get into the habit of brushing your cat's teeth, like you do your own, every day.

1. Scottish Fold Cat Health Concerns

A Scottish Fold cat will require a high amount of protein in their diet, as do most breeds of felines. You will help to ensure a long and healthy life by feeding them quality food. Look for food that lists meat as the first ingredient.

While a healthy spayed or neutered cat may live to be 10 to 12 years or more, and with proper care they may not suffer from any of the below noted health concerns, it is prudent to list all concerns that are possible, so that you have a clear understanding of problems that *"may"* affect your cat, including:

1) Degenerative Joint Disease: in the ankle and knee joints and especially in the tail, causing poor mobility and pain. If the cat has developed stiffness in their tail, it will be important to handle the tail very carefully.

2) Hypertrophic Cardiomyopathy: a form of heart disease has been seen in the breed, but it has not yet been proven to be a heritable form of the disease.

3) Polycystic Kidney Disease (PKD): this is an inherited disease that causes pockets of fluid to collect and grow in the cat's kidneys, which will eventually result in kidney failure. There is no specific treatment and depending upon the rate of growth a cat may show signs earlier or not until the age of 7 or older. Some cats may have PKD and still not suffer from kidney failure.

4) Osteochondrodysplasia (OCD): the forward folding ears of the Scottish Fold both define the breed and are the result of this debilitating condition, which is a developmental abnormality of the cartilage which would normally support the ear. Unfortunately, this abnormality also affects bone development and cartilage elsewhere in the cat's body.

How severely a cat is affected will depend upon whether one or both parents carry this mutated gene, for which there is no cure. This condition can be eliminated within a generation if breeding from cats with folded ears is stopped.

5) Obesity: without proper diet and exercise, any cat breed can become more prone to becoming obese, especially if they are an indoor cat. Indoor cats are certainly not going to be good candidates for "free feeding", as they will quickly become unhealthily overweight if you do not monitor their food intake.

Also, make sure that if this cat is not permitted outside, you provide him or her with plenty of fun ways to play and exercise, which will also help to keep their weight under control.

2. Allergies

One of the most common complaints discussed at the veterinarian's office when they see cats scratching and chewing at themselves is possible allergies.

Unlike us humans, who react to allergies with nasal symptoms, when our cats are suffering from allergies they will typically present itchy skin or ear problems.

a) Environmental Allergies

Allergies are usually first noticed because your cat is scratching, itching, biting, licking or chewing at their skin or paws.

Just like us humans, our cats can develop allergies to dust, chemicals, grass, mold, pollen, car exhaust, cigarette smoke, and flea and tick preparations, as well as allergies to materials such as wool or cotton, and chemicals found in washing soap or chemicals found in cleaning products you use around your home.

Symptoms are usually seen on the stomach, inside of the legs, and at the tail or paws.

Since most allergies are seasonal, our cats will be more affected in the spring or fall. Airborne irritants inhaled by your cat may result in coughing, sneezing or watery eyes.

If you think that your cat may have come in contact with an irritant found somewhere in your environment, the best thing to do for your cat is give them a cleansing bath, with the proper feline shampoo, followed by feline conditioner.

Remember that cats are closer to the ground, and the longer and softer their coat, the more they resemble a duster who attracts everything they come into contact with.

b) Food Allergies

"True" food allergies usually account for only about 10% of allergy problems in our feline friends.

For instance, itching, chewing and chronic ear infections are not actually caused by food allergies, but rather are the result of a suppressed immune system, which is caused by eating a low-quality diet.

These types of food allergies can often be completely resolved by changing your cat's diet to high-quality food that is more easily digested.

Proper nutrition is the easiest way to prevent any food allergies so if you want your cat to live a long and healthy life, don't cheap out on their very important food.

Many cat food products contain corn, wheat and soybeans, which are common allergens.

Usually it is the gluten in these foods that cause the allergic reaction which can show up at any age and our feline friends that are allergic to their food may display discomfort by scratching at their neck and head or may throw up their food or have diarrhea.

c) How to Diagnose a Food Allergy

Figuring out what food is causing an allergic reaction can be a challenging task and you will need to be a vigilant detective, because the only way to truly know which food is causing the troubles will be to introduce an elimination diet.

This means you will need to stop all treats and food and exclusively feed your cat a diet that you know is 100% free of allergy-causing ingredients, such as a hydrolyzed protein diet until all symptoms are no longer apparent. Be aware that this could take 10 to 12 weeks, depending on the particular cat and the severity of the allergic reaction.

Once all symptoms have vanished, you can then individually introduce treats or possibly offending foods to see which ones cause the allergic reaction.

Visit your local pet food store and educate yourself or talk with a knowledgeable representative because there's no excuse for feeding your cat a junk food diet when there are so many healthy choices now available that will help your feline companion live a long and healthy life.

Also keep in mind that our cats are constantly at risk for developing allergies because, beyond their food source, they are a small body being bombarded with many airborne irritants (herbicides, pesticides, vehicle exhaust, smoke, etc.) and often have toxic chemicals applied to their coat or ingested to prevent infestation of fleas.

As well, cats that are subjected to smoke from cigarettes or other sources can develop asthma.

d) Outside Dangers

Understandably, those cats that are not kept strictly indoors, who spend the majority of their time roaming about outdoors may be more prone to flea and pollen allergies or getting themselves into fights with neighborhood cats that can result in bodily injury from bites and scratches.

In addition, your cat may wander onto lawns or garden beds that have been doused with herbicides, pesticides or other toxic chemicals.

Further, if you live on a busy street, and your cat has access to the great outdoors, he or she may not make it home if they don't have sharp eyes, good hearing and strong road sense, because they can easily be accidentally struck and killed by a vehicle.

e) Flea Preparations – To Dose or Not to Dose

There is a growing concern amongst both the feline and feline lovers community that many so-called safe flea preparations are causing dangerous and life-threatening consequences.

Of course, our trusted veterinarians tell us that the topical flea preparations they are selling, such as *"Frontline"* costing $26 to $30 (£18 to £22) for a 3-month supply or the *"Soresto"* flea collar (lasting 8 months for a cost of $55 or £41), are safe even though the list of unpronounceable chemical ingredients is longer than your arm. These *"safe"* products also contain warnings that advise you to immediately wash your hands and not to let your children touch the cat after applying. Does this sound safe to you?

f) Safe Flea Prevention Alternatives

CedarCide – a 100% natural and safe product for use on everyone (even you). This family owned and operated business makes naturally sourced, highly effective alternatives to chemical-based pesticides for people, pets and homes.

Pet Protector – a 100% safe tag, that costs approximately $59.90 (£44.22) and lasts for four years, contains no chemicals or pesticides whatsoever, and your cat simply wears it on their collar.

This tag emits a charge with a specific combination of Magnetic and Scalar waves, which after being triggered by the animal's movement (blood circulation), produces an invisible energy field around the entire animal's body so that fleas and other crawly pests won't jump on board.

g) Cat Litter – the Bad and the Good

You might have previously believed that all cat litter is created equal, when the reality is that nothing could be farther from the truth. When you don't educate yourself and cheap out on the litter you buy for your cat's box, you may be inadvertently creating a health problem for your cat and yourself, not to mention the environment.

You need to be aware that many mass-produced cat litters can cause upper respiratory distress to your cat (and yourself), because they contain high amounts of silica dust.

Also, many manufacturers add a lovely perfumed scent to the litter they produce, because this appeals to the sensitive noses of us humans by helping to disguise the smell of urine and cat feces, and this scent is usually derived from toxic chemicals that can also be harmful to your cat.

Further, those clumping litters containing sodium bentonite can cause several problems, including:

- the litter can swell up to 15 times its original volume and when a cat is cleaning their feet, they can ingest some of this litter, which can cause gastrointestinal distress that, if severe enough, can lead to death.

- the type of clay that is used for the manufacturing of clumping litter is usually obtained through an environmentally destructive strip mining process.

h) Greener Cat Litter Choices

Thankfully, we humans are finally starting to realize how much our choices for our pets can be adversely impacting their health and the environment where we live, and this means that we are choosing healthier alternatives.

It's up to you to make greener and healthier choices for yourself, your cat and your environment.

For instance, a non-toxic, unscented option for you might be *"Yesterday's News"*, which is a cat litter made from dust-free, recycled newspaper that is more absorbent than clay-based products.

There are many other healthy cat litter choices out there and if you are concerned about your cat's health, you need to research greener cat litter choices, such as:

"Cedarific Natural Cat Litter", a dust-free, inexpensive blend of cedar and hardwood chips that has a pleasant cedar odor and is both biodegradable and compostable

"Feline Pine", made from dust-free pine chips

"Better Way Cat Litter", naturally controls odor with a combination of clay and cedar chips

"Eco-Shells Purr and Simple Cat Litter", made from a blend of tree nut fibrous material

"Swheat Scoop Natural Wheat Litter", made from renewable wheat crops, uses natural enzymes to remove odours

"World's Best Cat Litter", made from whole kernel corn

3. Saving Your Cat With CPR

Of course, nobody wants to ever be put in a situation where the life of their precious feline companion is at risk, however, the reality is that accidents happen, and therefore knowing a little bit about how to help save your beloved furry friend is time well spent.

First of all, remember to handle an injured cat very carefully and gently. A cat that is traumatized, fearful or in pain, even one that is usually gentle, may lash out and try to bite.

Consider taking a class, because there are many animal CPR courses being offered these days through community educational systems or even online.

It's also a good idea to have a feline first aid kit both at home and in your vehicle in case of emergencies. Items to keep handy in your first aid kit may include:

- Scissors
- Tweezers
- Tick Twister
- Nail Scissors
- Kwik Stop Styptic powder
- Gauze bandaging
- Non-stick bandages for wounds
- Medical tape
- Antiseptic wash for wounds (hydrogen peroxide)
- Sterile eyewash
- Towel
- Washcloth

- Blanket

Artificial Respiration Step by Step

If your cat becomes unconscious, depending upon what happened to them, they may stop breathing and if they stop breathing, what comes next will be cardiac arrest, when the heart stops beating and the cat dies.

However, after breathing stops and before cardiac arrest, the heart can continue to beat for several minutes and this is when performing cardiopulmonary resuscitation (CPR) or artificial respiration can save your cat's life.

Step 1: place your cat on his or her side on a flat surface.

Step 2: check to make sure that your cat has actually stopped breathing by watching for the rise and fall of their chest and feel for their breath on your hand. Check the color of your cat's gums because lack of oxygen will make them turn blue.

Step 3: check that the cat's airway is clear and there is nothing stuck in their mouth or throat by extending the head and neck and opening your cat's mouth.

If there is an object blocking their throat, pull the tongue outward and use your fingers or pliers to get a firm grip on the object, so that you can pull it free from the cat's throat.

If you cannot reach an object that appears to be blocking the cat's airway passage, you will have to use the Heimlich manoeuvre to try and dislodge it.

Step 4: so long as the cat's airway is not blocked, you can lift the cat's chin to straighten out the neck and begin rescue breathing.

Step 5: hold the cat's muzzle and close their mouth, put your mouth over the cat's nose and blow gently – just enough to cause the cat's chest to rise.

Step 6: wait long enough for the air you just breathed into the cat's lungs to leave before giving another breath.

Step 7: continue giving one gentle breath every 3 seconds as long as the heart is still beating and until your cat starts to breathe on their own.

CPR Step by Step

If your cat's heart has stopped beating, then CPR must be started immediately and ideal would be to have one person performing the artificial respiration while the other performs the CPR.

Step 1: put your cat on his or her side on a flat surface.

Step 2: feel for your cat's pulse or heartbeat by placing one hand over his or her left side, just behind the front leg.

Step 3: place the palm of your hand on your cat's rib cage over his or her heart, with your other hand on top of the first (for kittens, put just your thumb on one side of the chest and the rest of your fingers on the other side).

Step 4: press down and release, compressing the cat's chest approximately one inch (2.5 centimetres) and squeeze and release 80 to 100 times every minute.

Chapter 11: Daily Feeding & Care

1. Feeding Kittens

For growing kittens with small stomachs, a general rule of thumb is to feed them smaller meals at least four times a day so that they receive the proper amount of nutrients.

You will have to decide what food you want to feed your kitten and eventually your cat and if you are serious about raising a healthy kitten that has the best opportunity of living a long life, you will want to educate yourself about the vast differences in quality of food, so that you realize that making the wrong choices can mean the beginning of many health issues for your cat.

Make sure that you read Chapter 13 (Medical Care and Safety, under Obesity) that contains valuable information about appropriate food choices for your cat.

When you kitten is around six months old, you can begin to reduce their feeding schedule to three times a day.

While some kittens will continue to grow after one year, cats are generally considered to be full grown at one year of age, at which time you can reduce their feeding schedule to twice daily.

There are now many foods on the market that are formulated for all stages of a cat's life (including the kitten stage), and you will want to keep in mind that cats would normally eat a meat-based diet if they could choose for themselves.

2. Feeding the Adult Scottish Fold Cat

An adult cat will generally need to be fed twice a day, and you will want to carefully read the labels and avoid foods that contain a high amount of grains and other fillers in favor of foods that list high quality meat protein as the main ingredient.

Keep in mind that every cat is unique and your cat may or may not be as active as some other breeds. Many cats are not good candidates for "free feeding" (especially if they are indoor cats), which means that you may have to carefully monitor their food intake.

Picky Eaters: be careful that you do not get into the habit of "doctoring" your cat's food with bits and pieces of your human food, otherwise you will inadvertently create a picky eater who will then refuse to eat.

It is important that your cat understands that you are in control of their food source, and once they understand this, they will also understand that they have a certain amount of time in which to eat their food.

3. Cat Food and Treats

Since the creation of the first cat food (late 1800's) over 120 years ago, the myriad of choices available in every pet store, feed store and grocery store shelf almost outnumbers those looking forward to eating them.

While considered mostly a luxury until the 1920's, some believe that Ralston Purina was the first company to commercially produce cat food and Gaines Food was the first to introduce canned cat food. The commercial cat food industry really began to take off during the 1900s.

What has evolved to become known as *"cat food"* today was a 20th century development, that took advantage of creating a very large income out of food that would otherwise have been delegated to the local landfill.

Just like cat food, cat treats need to be chosen with the health of your kitten or cat in mind, rather than the convenience of one-stop shopping at your local grocery store that may tend to have less than healthy choices.

Today's treats are not just for making us feel better, because it makes us happy to give our furry friends something they really enjoy; today's treats are also designed to actually improve our cat's health.

Some of us humans treat our cats just because, others use treats for training purposes or bribes, others for health, while others treat for a combination of reasons.

Whatever reason you choose to give treats to your cat, keep in mind that if we treat our cats too often throughout the day, we may create a picky eater who will no longer want to eat their regular meals.

As well, if the treats we are giving are high calorie, we may be putting our cat's health in jeopardy by allowing them to become overweight.

4. Healthy Treats

a) Raw Chicken Organs: if your family eats chicken, save the organs or giblets for your cat that will appreciate the organ meat as a tasty treat.

b) Freeze Dried: many healthy, one-ingredient treats are freeze-dried (chicken, beef, sardines, shrimp) and easy to feed as treats to your cat.

c) Feeder Mice or Chicks: while you may be feeling squeamish about feeding frozen baby mice or chicks as treats to your cat, you cannot deny that if they were hunting in the wild, this is what they would be eating and that these "treats" provide the bones, meat, muscle and organs your cat needs.

There are now many healthy choices in both food and treats for your cat, that are far superior to what was considered "good" for our cats in the past, so there is no excuse for not feeding your cat healthy treats.

5. Choosing the Right Food

In order to choose the right food for your cat, first it's important to understand a little bit about feline physiology and what Mother Nature intended when she created our fur friends.

Out of the meager beginning of the first commercially made cat food has sprung a massively lucrative and vastly confusing industry that has only recently begun to evolve beyond those early days of feeding our cats the dregs of human leftovers, because it was cheap and convenient for us.

Even today, many cat food choices have far more to do with being convenient for humans to store and serve, than it does with being a diet truly designed to be a nutritionally balanced, healthy food choice for a feline.

The pet food industry is very big business and as such, because there are now almost limitless choices, there is much confusion and endless debate when it comes to answering the question, *"What is the best food for my cat?"*

Educating yourself by talking to experts and reading everything you can find on the subject, plus taking into consideration several relevant factors, will help to answer the cat food question for you and your cat.

For instance, where you live may dictate what sorts of foods you have access to. Other factors to consider will include the particular requirements of your cat, such as their age, energy and activity levels.

Next will be expense, time and quality. While we all want to give our cats the best food possible, many humans lead very busy lives and cannot, for instance, prepare their own cat food, but still want to feed a high-quality diet that fits within their budget.

However, perhaps most important when choosing an appropriate diet for our cats is learning to be more observant of Mother Nature's design and taking a closer look at our cat's teeth, jaws and digestive tract in order to truly understand what is best for our cats.

While humans are herbivores who derive energy from eating plants, our feline companions are carnivores, which means that they derive their energy and nutrient requirements from eating a diet consisting mainly or exclusively of the flesh of animal tissues (in other words, meat).

a) The Feline Teeth: the first part of your cat you will want to take a good look at when considering what to feed will be their teeth.

Unlike humans, who are equipped with wide, flat molars for grinding grains, vegetables and other plant-based materials, feline teeth are all pointed, because they are designed to rip, shred and tear into animal meat and bone.

b) The Feline Jaw: another obvious consideration when choosing an appropriate food source is the fact that every feline is born equipped with powerful jaws and neck muscles for the specific purpose of being able to pull down and tear apart their hunted prey.

The structure of the jaw of every feline is such that it opens widely to hold large pieces of meat and bone, while the actual mechanics of a cat's jaw permits only vertical (up and down) movement that is designed for crushing.

c) The Feline Digestive Tract: a cat's digestive tract is short and simple and designed to move their natural choice of food (hide, meat and bone) quickly through their systems.

Given the choice, most cats would never choose to eat plants or vegetables and fruits over meat, however, we continue to feed them a kibble-based diet that often can contain high amounts of vegetables, fruits and grains and low amounts of meat.

How much healthier and long-lived might our beloved friends be if, instead of largely ignoring nature's design for our feline companions, we chose to feed them whole, unprocessed, species-appropriate food?

With many hundreds of cat food brands to choose from, it's no wonder we humans are confused about what to feed our cats to help them live long and healthy lives. The following are some suggestions and questions that may help you choose a cat food company that you can feel comfortable with:

- How long have they have been in business?
- Is cat food their main industry?
- Are they dedicated to their brand?
- Are they easily accessible?
- Do they honestly answer your questions?
- Do they have a good Company Safety Standard?
- Do they set higher standards?

- Read the ingredients - where did they come from?
- Are the ingredients something you would eat?
- Are the ingredients farmed locally?
- Was it cooked using standards you would trust?
- Is the company certified under human food or organic guidelines?

Whatever you decide to feed your cat, keep in mind that, just as too much wheat, other grains and other fillers in our human diet is having detrimental effects on our health, the same can be very true for our pets.

Our cats are also suffering from many of the same life-threatening diseases that are commonly found in our human society (heart disease, cancer, diabetes, obesity), which all have a direct correlation with eating genetically altered foods that are no longer pure, in favor of a convenient, processed and packaged diet.

6. The Raw Diet

While more and more of us humans are coming to the belief that we are killing ourselves and our cats with processed foods, others believe that there are dangers involved in feeding raw foods to our fur friends.

Those who are raw feeding advocates believe that the ideal diet for their cat is one which would be very similar to what a cat living in the wild would have access to hunting or foraging, and these feline guardians are often opposed to feeding their cat any sort of commercially manufactured pet foods, because they consider them to be poor substitutes.

On the other hand, those opposed to feeding their cats a raw or biologically appropriate raw food diet believe that the risks associated with food-borne illnesses, during the handling and feeding of raw meats, outweigh the purported benefits.

Raw meats purchased at your local grocery store may contain a much higher level of acceptable bacteria than raw food produced for cats, because the meat purchased for human consumption is supposed to be cooked, which will kill any bacteria that might be present.

This means that feline guardians feeding their cats a raw food diet can be quite certain that commercially prepared raw foods sold in pet stores will be safer than raw meats purchased in grocery stores.

Many educated people who have taken the time to do the research, will agree that their cats thrive on a raw diet and strongly believe that the potential benefits of feeding a raw cat food diet are many, including:

- Healthy, shiny coats
- Decreased shedding
- Fewer allergy problems
- Healthier skin
- Cleaner teeth
- Fresher breath
- Increased energy levels
- Improved digestion
- Smaller stools
- Strengthened immune system
- Increased mobility in arthritic pets
- Increase or improvement in overall health

All cats of every size, are amazing athletes in their own right, therefore every cat deserves to be fed the best food available.

A raw diet is a direct evolution of what cats ate before they became our domesticated pets and we turned toward commercially prepared, easy to serve dry cat food that required no special storage or preparation.

A biologically appropriate raw diet is all about feeding our cats what they are designed to eat by returning them to their wild, evolutionary diet.

7. The Dehydrated Diet

Dehydrated cat food comes in both raw meat and cooked meat forms and these foods are usually air dried to reduce moisture to the level where bacterial growth is inhibited.

The appearance of dehydrated cat food is very similar to dry kibble and the typical feeding methods include adding warm water before serving, which makes this type of diet both healthy for our cats and convenient for us to serve.

Dehydrated recipes are made from minimally processed fresh whole foods to create a healthy and nutritionally balanced meal that will meet or exceed the dietary requirements of a healthy feline.

Dehydrating removes only the moisture from the fresh ingredients, which usually means that because the food has not already been cooked at a high temperature, more of the overall nutrition is retained.

A dehydrated diet is a convenient way to feed your cat a nutritious diet, because all you have to do is add warm water and wait five minutes while the food re-hydrates so your cat can enjoy a warm meal.

8. The Kibble Diet

While many feline guardians are starting to take a closer look at the food choices they are making for their furry companions, there is no mistaking that the convenience and relative economy of dry cat food kibble, which had its beginnings during the 1900's, continues to be the most popular pet food choice for many cat-friendly humans.

Now, the massive pet food industry offers up a confusingly large number of choices with hundreds of different manufacturers and brand names lining the shelves of veterinarian offices, grocery stores and pet food aisles.

NOTE: as a general rule of thumb, the best pet foods are NOT found in the grocery isle of your local supermarket.

Take the time to buy your food from a trusted pet store and be sure to carefully read the labels, so that you are not feeding your beloved fur friend an inferior food that could be harmful to their health.

While feeding a high quality bagged kibble diet that has been flavored to appeal to cats and supplemented with vegetables and fruits to appeal to humans may keep most feline companions happy and relatively healthy, you will ultimately need to decide whether this is the best diet for them.

9. The Right Bowl

Here is a brief description of the different categories and types of bowls that would be appropriate choices for your cat's particular needs.

Automatic Food or Watering Bowls: are standard cat bowls (often made out of plastic) that are attached to a reservoir container, which is designed to keep food dispensed on a timer and water constantly available to your cat as long as there is water remaining in the storage compartment.

Ceramic/Stoneware Bowls: an excellent choice for those who like options in personality, color and shape.

Elevated Bowls: raised dining table cat bowls are a tidy and classy choice that will make your cat's dinner time a more comfortable experience while getting the bowls off the floor.

No Skid Bowls: are for cats that push their bowls across the floor when eating. A non-skid cat bowl will help keep the food bowl where you put it.

No Tip Bowls: are designed to prevent the messy type of eater from playing with their food or flipping over their dinner or water bowls.

Stainless Steel Bowls: are as close to indestructible as a bowl can be, plus they are sanitary, easy to clean and water stays cooler for a longer period of time in a stainless bowl.

Travel Bowls: are convenient, practical and handy additions for every feline travel kit.

Consider a space saving, collapsible cat bowl, made out of hygienic, renewable bamboo that comes in fun colors and different sizes, making them perfect for travelling with your feline friend.

10. Exercise

All of our feline companions are amazing, natural athletes and because of this, they need daily exercise to stay fit, happy and healthy and just because they may be an indoor cat, doesn't mean that they should become an overweight couch potato.

Almost every cat will require daily exercise to stay happy and healthy. They will love playing enticing games or interacting with other pets in your home.

Any type of interactive exercise you can engage in with your cat will help to exercise both their body and their intelligent mind and will burn off pent-up daily energy reserves so that your cat will be a happy and contented companion.

All cats like to climb and observe their domain from a higher vantage point, so make sure you give them this opportunity by providing them with a cat tree and a scratching post for healthy stretching, so they don't use your favorite couch for sharpening their claws.

Cats must maintain their claws and the only way they can do that is by scratching, which helps remove dead nail growth and also marks their territory (there are scent glands on the paws).

11. Playtime

Every cat needs some regular playtime each day, and while every cat will be different with respect to what types of games they may enjoy, most will really love any game involving chasing a string or toy that appears to be alive.

12. Daily Grooming

Daily grooming is a must for any healthy cat, so make sure that you get into the routine of spending at least 5 minutes each day brushing or combing your cat, checking their ears and nails and brushing their teeth.

13. Safe Traveling

Far too many feline guardians do nothing to protect their companions when traveling with them inside their vehicles and some cities are fining vehicle operators for allowing their pets to roam freely inside their moving vehicle, because this is considered distracted driving.

There is no denying that cats that are not properly restrained become projectiles in any sort of vehicle crash and if involved in an accident, the cat can be seriously injured or killed if they are thrown through a window.

If you opt to contain your best friend inside a kennel or crate, you absolutely must make sure that the kennel is very securely attached with the vehicle's seatbelt system.

A hard-sided cat kennel or crate will easily fit (sideways) on the back seat of most vehicles and can be secured with the vehicle's restraint system, and a cat riding inside a kennel that is secure inside your vehicle will have the best protection in the case of a rollover accident.

Keep in mind that some cities are now fining drivers for allowing an animal to be freely roaming about the inside of a moving vehicle, and if you get your cat used to safely traveling inside a kennel inside your vehicle, you will avoid these fines.

As well, there are many soft kennel manufacturers, such as Sleepypod (that has a #1 safety rating), and can be securely attached to your vehicles seatbelt system.

Keep your cat safe when traveling in your vehicle. Do your research and transport your cat inside a kennel with a good safety rating that is both strength tested and certified to be able to keep your cat safe in the event of an accident.

The Scottish Fold will usually be small enough to travel comfortably inside a Sherpa bag inside the airplane cabin as a kitten or when they are full grown, and can be *"carry on baggage"* if the carrier conforms to the airline regulations, which state that a pet carrier must be able to fit under the seat in front of you.

If you plan to regularly travel with your cat, get them used to their Sherpa bag when they are kittens so they will not fear it or think that the only time they travel in the carrier is followed by a stressful visit to the vet's office.

Most soft carriers are airline approved and under-seat dimensions are generally as follows:

- Window Seat: 19" L x 14" W x 8.25" H
- [48.26 cm L x 35.56 cm W x 20.955 cm H]

- Middle Seat: 19" L x 19" W x 8.25" H
- [48.26 cm L x 48.26 cm W x 20.955 cm H]

- Aisle Seat: 19" L x 14" W x 8.25" H
- [48.26 cm L x 35.56 cm W x 20.955 cm H]

For in-cabin travel by plane, your kitten or cat must be able to stand up and turn around comfortably inside the bag. Airlines also require an absorbent liner in the bag, which could be a pee pad, an old towel, a favorite blanket, or a cosy, faux lambskin liner.

Many styles of feline carrier bags are officially approved for airline travel, and when you make your flight reservations, don't forget to reserve for your kitten or cat as well, because there is generally a small charge for in-cabin travel and some airlines will only permit a certain number of feline travellers per flight.

Any kitten or cat that is too large to fit inside a Sherpa bag will need to be transported inside a securely fastened, hard-sided kennel inside the airplane cargo hold.

Chapter 12: Scottish Fold Cat Training Advice

1. Human Training

House training, *"potty"*, *"litter box"* or *"toilet"* training is a critical first step in the education of any new kitten, and the first part of a successful process is training the human guardian.

When you bring home your new kitten, they will be relying on your guidance to teach them what they might not have already learned from their mother.

When you provide your kitten with your consistent patience and understanding, they are capable of learning rules at a very early age, and house training is no different, especially since it's all about establishing a regular routine.

If you learn to pay attention, house training a new kitten can be quick and effortless — how quick depends entirely upon you. Make sure your energy remains consistently calm and patient and that you exercise plenty of compassion and understanding while you help your new kitten learn their new bathroom rules.

The first step will be to establish a daily routine that will work well for both feline and human alike, and depending upon the age of your kitten, make a plan to take them to their designated potty area at least every two hours and stick to it. While you are in the beginning stages of training, the more vigilant and consistent you can be, the quicker and more successful your results will be.

2. Litter Box Training

Most cat guardians opt for the litter box when potty training their kitten, as kittens and cats naturally choose this type of bathroom routine even when they have access to the great outdoors.

Being naturally fastidious, cats will easily learn to use a litter box for their bathroom routine and it will not take very much encouragement to teach them how to do this.

Simply place your kitten in the litter box that is lined with the appropriate amount of fresh litter and your cat will quickly get the idea.

Generally speaking, while how many times during the day a cat may need to void their bladder will vary between cats and how much they drink during the day, on average most cats will need to empty their bladder at least every 8 to 12 hours.

A young kitten will be able to hold their bladder and bowels for shorter periods of time and after a kitten eats food or drinks, they generally may have to relieve themselves within 10 minutes and some of the first indications or signs that your kitten needs to relieve themselves will be when you see them:

- Sniffing around
- Looking for the litter box or bathroom
- Acting agitated or crying at a door to get out
- Kittens and cats squat before urinating
- If you notice your kitten squatting, immediately take him or her to their litter box or toilet area

- Be aware that if a kitten cannot easily find the right place to go to the bathroom, they may choose a soft carpet, towel or even your shoes for relieving themselves

Initially, treats can be a good way to reinforce how pleased you are that your kitten is learning to go potty in the right place, and then the treats can be slowly removed and replaced with your happy praise.

Next, now that you have a new kitten in your life, you will want to be flexible with respect to adapting your schedule to meet the requirements that will help to quickly teach your kitten their new bathroom routine.

This means not leaving your kitten alone for endless hours at a time because firstly, they need companionship and your direction when they are still growing kittens, plus long periods alone will result in the disruption of the potty training schedule you have worked hard to establish.

If you have no choice but to leave your kitten alone for many hours, make sure that you place them in the bathroom or a room that has the litter box area already established.

Remember, a growing kitten has a bladder and bowels that they do not yet have complete control over and you will have a much happier time and better success if you simply train yourself to pay attention to when your young companion is showing signs of needing to relieve themselves.

Often the situation of cats relieving themselves in the wrong place can be avoided if their human guardian is paying attention.

3. Toilet Training

While litter box training is quite simple and easy, if you don't relish the idea of buying truck loads of cat litter and scooping and disposing of soiled litter over the life of your cat, you might want to take a little longer with the potty training routine and instead teach your cat to use the toilet, especially since it's not that difficult to do.

While there are varying trains of thought about training a cat to use the human toilet, there are training devices out there designed to help train an adult cat to use the toilet instead of a litter box (Litter Kwitter or CitiKitty) and you will have to decide whether you want to go this route with your cat.

If you are determined to teach your cat to use the toilet, it might be a good idea to have a second bathroom set up just for the cat, so that humans and cats don't have to share a toilet.

4. Bell Training

If you have an outdoor cat that is used to going outside to relieve his or herself, you might want to teach them to ring a bell to let you know when they need to go out.

Attach the bell to a piece of ribbon or string and hang it from a door handle or tape it to a doorsill near the door where you will be letting them out when they need to relieve themselves and show them how to use their paw to ring the bell. Praise them for this *"trick"* and immediately open the door, when they ring the bell.

The only downside to teaching your kitten or cat to ring a bell when they want to go outside is that even if they don't actually have to go out to relieve themselves, but just want to go outside because they are bored, you will still have to open the door every time they ring the bell.

There are many types and styles of *"gotta go"* commercially manufactured bells you could choose, ranging from the elegant "Poochie Bells" that hang from a doorknob, the simple "Tell Bell" that sits on the floor, or various high-tech door chime systems that function much like an intercom system, where they push a pad with their paw and it rings a bell.

While these types of bell systems were initially designed for the canine companion, there is no reason why the clever cat can't also learn to ring a bell when they need to go out.

Whatever doorbell system you choose for your kitten or cat, once they are trained, this type of an alert system is an easy way to eliminate accidents at home.

5. Cat Door

If you decide that you want your cat to be able to let his or herself in and outside whenever they wish, you might want to install a cat door or cat flap in one of your doors leading to the outside.

Once you have installed the cat flap, you will need to first lift the flap and show your kitten or cat that this is an exit to the outside and then gently push your cat through the door a few times until they realize how it works.

If you have a friend to help you, they can be on the other side of the flap with a treat, to help entice your kitten to push itself through the flap.

6. Kennel Training

Kennel training is always a good idea for any kitten early in their education, because it can be utilized for many different situations, including keeping them safe while traveling inside a vehicle when being transported to the vet's office or any time you have to travel with them.

When purchasing a kennel for your kitten, always buy a kennel that will be the correct size for your kitten once they grow into adulthood.

The kennel will be the correct size if your adult cat can stand up and easily turn around inside their kennel.

When you train your kitten to accept sleeping in their own kennel at night time, this may also help to accelerate their potty training, because no kitten or cat wants to relieve themselves where they sleep, which means that they will hold their bladder and bowels as long as they possibly can.

Be watchful and consistent so that you learn your kitten's body language, and listen to their meows, which will alert you to when it's time for them to use the litter box, toilet or great outdoors.

7. Free Training

If you would rather not confine your young kitten to one or two rooms in your home and will be allowing them to freely range about your home anywhere they wish during the day, this is considered free training.

When free potty training your kitten, you will need to closely watch your kitten's activities all day long so that you can be aware of the *"signs"* that will indicate when they need to relieve themselves. For instance, circling and sniffing or crying may be a sure sign that they are looking for a place to do their business.

Never get upset or scold a kitten for having an accident inside the home, because this will result in teaching your kitten to be afraid of you and to only relieve themselves in secret places or when you're not watching.

If you catch your kitten making a mistake, all that is necessary is for you to calmly say *"No"*, and quickly scoop them up and take them to their permitted bathroom area.

When you are vigilant, most kittens are not difficult to housebreak and they will generally do very well when you start them off with a litter box. If you are going to train them to use the toilet or go outside, simply move the litter box slowly closer to the door you want them to go out, or area you want to eventually be their bathroom.

When you pay close attention to your kitten's sleeping, eating, drinking and playing habits, you will quickly learn their body language so that you are able to predict when they might need to relieve themselves.

Your kitten will usually need to relieve themselves first thing in the morning, as soon as they wake up from a nap, approximately 10 minutes after they finish eating a meal or drinking after they have finished a play session.

It's important to have compassion during this house training time in your young cat's life, so that their education will be as stress-free as possible.

It's also important to be vigilant because how well you pay attention will minimize the opportunities your kitten may have for making a bathroom mistake in the first place, and the fewer mistakes they make, the sooner your kitten will be house trained.

8. Mistakes Happen

Remember that a domestic cat's sense of smell is approximately 14 times more sensitive than the human sense of smell, because they have twice the "smell-sensitive" cells in their noses, which means their sense of smell is considerably more acute than it is for us humans.

As a result, it will be very important to effectively remove all odors from house training accidents, because otherwise your kitten will be attracted by the smell to the place where they may have had a previous accident and will want to do their business there again and again.

As well, if you are using a litter box and it is not regularly cleaned, your cat or kitten may refuse to use it.

While there are many products that are supposed to remove odors and stains, many of them are not particularly effective because they simply mask one odor with another scent, when what you really need is a product that will completely neutralize the offending odors.

For instance, a company called "Remove Urine Odors" has a product called *"SUN"* and another product called *"Max Enzyme"*, both of which contain professional-strength odor neutralizers and urine digesters that bind to and completely absorb odors on any type of surface.

9. Electronic Training Devices

Generally speaking, while positive training methods can be more effective than using devices that involve negative stimulation, cats tend to be more independent minded and athletic than the average dog, which means you may need to avail yourself of the assistance that electronic training devices can supply.

If you have a stubborn cat that insists on walking through their litter box and then jumping up on your kitchen counter where you prepare food for yourself and your family, you might want to find a method that will more effectively dissuade them from this unhygienic practice.

Scat Mat

For instance, there is a product called *"Scat Mat"*, which is available in several different sizes of mats and strips and designed to teach your cat good manners and to stay away from certain areas by emitting a mild, harmless 3-second static pulse any time the cat touches the mat.

Invisible Fencing?

If you want to let your cat out into your own back yard and are worried that they may stray farther, some might want to consider installing an invisible fence and while this sounds like a reasonable solution, most cats, when intent on pursuing a bird or other enticing prey, will ignore the shock they receive when running through the invisible perimeter of an electric fence.

Worse might be that once on the other side of the "fence", the cat will remember the shock they received and be afraid to return home.

10. Yard Safety

Of course, our cats ideally want to be outside where they can smell the air, hear and see birds and other sounds of the natural world, but we all know that cats live longer when they are not permitted to roam freely outdoors, so what's the solution?

If you have a back yard, you might want to consider an outdoor cat enclosure, which will provide your cat with the best of both worlds by keeping them and the birds and wildlife that might frequent your garden safe and healthy.

The only way to absolutely ensure that your cat remains safe and out of harm in their own back yard is to secure them inside an outdoor enclosure, playpen or cat patio.

There are many manufacturers of outdoor enclosures such as what can be found at *"Catio Spaces",* and a little research will reveal that there are many styles and configurations to choose from that may range in price from $200 to $2,000 (£148 to £1,477) depending upon how large or elaborate you want the structure to be, and what materials it may be constructed with.

Chapter 13: Medical Care & Safety

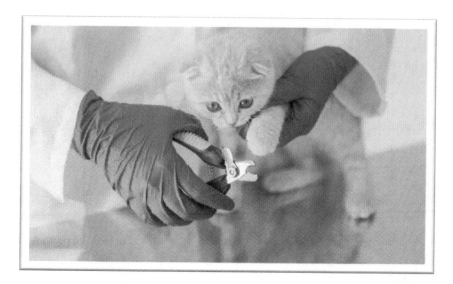

1. Choosing a Veterinarian

A consideration to keep in mind when choosing a veterinarian clinic will be that some clinics specialize in caring for smaller pets, and some specialize in larger animal care, while still others have a wide-ranging area of expertise and will care for all animals, including livestock and reptiles.

Choosing a clinic will be a personal decision, however, your cat's needs may be better served by choosing a clinic that specializes in the care of smaller domesticated pets or even one that is exclusively for cats.

Choosing a good veterinary clinic will be very similar to choosing the right health care clinic or doctor for your own personal health, because you want to ensure that your kitten receives the quality care he or she deserves. Begin your search by asking other cat owners where they take their furry friends and whether they are happy with the service they receive.

If you don't know anyone to ask, visit a few local pet stores in your area as they should be able to provide you with references and local listings of pet care clinics.

Next, check online, because a good pet clinic will have an active website up and running that will list current details of all the services they provide along with an overview of all staff members, their education and qualifications.

Once you've narrowed your search, it's time to personally visit the clinics you may be interested in, as this will be a good opportunity for you and your kitten to visually inspect the facility, interact with the staff and perhaps meet the veterinarians face to face.

Of course, it's not just you who needs to feel comfortable with the clinic chosen and those working there. Your kitten needs to feel comfortable, too, and this is where visiting a clinic and interacting with the staff and veterinarians will provide you with an idea of their experience and expertise in handling cats and kittens.

If your kitten or cat is comfortable with them, then you will be much more likely to trust that they will be providing the best care for your kitten who will need to receive all his or her vaccinations and yearly check-ups, and eventually be spayed or neutered.

It's also a good idea to take your kitten into your chosen clinic several times before they actually need to be there for any treatment, so that they are not fearful of the new smells and unfamiliar surroundings.

2. Vaccinations

Always make sure that you carry out extensive research with respect to vaccinations, how much and how often your cat actually needs them.

For instance, do you understand what vaccines actually are and why your pet needs them? Be aware that, just like the human drug industry, the pet vaccine industry is very BIG business that could reach $7.2 billion (£5.2 billion) by the year 2020.

First of all, the purpose of vaccines is to hyper-stimulate a healthy cat's immune system so that it will develop an immune response to a particular bacteria, infection or virus, and this sounds safe, doesn't it?

Yes and no, because it seems that there is much new research being carried out proving that vaccinations are also causing many of our beloved pets to get sick and even die.

Of course, we want to protect our cats from deadly diseases, such as distemper and rabies, but do we ever stop to consider the side effects?

Vaccinating a Healthy Cat

Did you know that every vaccination pamphlet produced clearly states, *"Only vaccinate a healthy animal"?* Yet, how many animals are being vaccinated despite the fact that they are suffering from allergies, cancers and other issues? The answer is, *"far too many"*.

All At Once?

There is also mounting evidence to prove that a combination vaccinating routine is causing massive overstimulation of the cat's immune system.

You don't really need to be a scientist to understand that giving more than one vaccine at a time will obviously cause more adverse side effects and that the smaller the patient (cat or dog), the more likely they will be faced with an adverse reaction.

There have been studies carried out on cats and dogs, both of which reached the same conclusion – vaccines should not be given together.

Despite the conclusion reached by these studies, there are five viral diseases that cats are commonly vaccinated against, which are often administered at the same time (called "FVRCP", which includes Rhinotracheitis, Calci, Panleukopenia, Feline Leukemia and Rabies).

The Rabies Law

Yes, there actually is a law that says you must take your cat or dog to your veterinarian to have them vaccinated against the deadly rabies virus every three years, whether or not they need it.

Guess what? If a blood test is carried out and there are circulating antibodies present, your pet doesn't need another rabies vaccine and in 99% of all cases, a one-time rabies vaccination is good for the life of the pet.

Would you submit to having a rabies vaccination every year, especially if you knew it could make you sick? I think not.

Further, it is still the law to give a 2-pound (0.9 kg) Chihuahua the same "full" rabies dose as is given to a 200-pound (90.7 kg) Great Dane, and the same holds true for a cat, which is much smaller.

How does this make any logical sense, especially when it is known that many of our beloved pets are dying from this? There is no question that this law needs to be changed.

Tumors and Cancer

Quite simply said by Dr. Patricia Jordan (a 1986 graduate of the North Carolina College of Veterinary Medicine), *"Vaccines have cancer-causing viruses in them"*.

For instance, there is evidence showing that an infectious feline leukemia virus has been part of the master vaccine seed stock that is routinely given to cats and other pets.

There is now documented evidence that it is quite common for tumors to grow at the site of the vaccinations and that sometimes these tumors are not just little bumps – they are very large and they are referred to as *"vaccine associated sarcomas"*.

The word *"sarcoma"* means cancer that has occurred as a result of transformed cells and when these tumors are dissected, there is irrefutable evidence that they are caused by the vaccine itself, because remnants of the vaccine are found at the centre of the tumor.

Retroviruses

What many humans also don't know about vaccines is that as a result of the manufacturing process, where they mix and mingle different animal cells together, they contain retroviruses than can literally alter the DNA of an animal.

While some may not cause harm, others can severely compromise the immune system of an animal, which will eventually lead to cancer.

What's worse is that this is an area of the vaccine industry that has yet to even be addressed.

This means that our favorite fur friends are constantly being contaminated and end up being expendable guinea pigs for the vaccine manufacturers and we are left with sick pets as a result of an exploding growth of many types of cancers being seen in our animal population.

Autoimmune Diseases

There was a study carried out at Purdue, which is a major research university in Indiana, proving that there is an autoimmune disease link to vaccinations.

When there is break down of the autoimmune system and it becomes compromised, this will eventually lead to a wide variety of disorders, including cancer and heart disease.

Over-Vaccination

Tumors are just one problem that can occur from vaccinations, because for as long as I can remember we humans have been told that we need to have our dogs and cats re-vaccinated every single year. Really? Let's use common sense here and ask ourselves: do we humans get ourselves vaccinated every single year? Of course, we don't.

It's apparently been known in the veterinarian world since 1945 that it only takes one vaccination to protect a mature mammal for life. There is also much documented evidence from some of the world's leading doctors and immunologists, who agree there is an epidemic of *"rampant over-vaccinating"* of our beloved cats and dogs, indicating evidence that yearly vaccines are causing cancer.

So, while we humans are dutifully taking our cats and dogs to the vet every year for their booster shots, thinking we are doing our best for them, we may in actuality be causing them to develop cancer and die prematurely.

Unfortunately, just like our human medical doctors, when veterinarians are in school, they are taught a *"pattern of medicine"* that if strictly adhered to can actually become quite toxic for our fur friends.

We need to be aware, educate ourselves, use common sense, and ask questions if we are going to give our cats and dogs their best chance at a long and healthy life. For instance, there is a textbook called *"Current Veterinary Therapy"* containing an article written by two veterinary immunologists back in 1992, which states: *"the practice of annual revaccination is lacking in scientific merit"*.

Thankfully, more veterinarian practices are nowadays suggesting the alternative of a much safer blood test, called *"vaccine titer testing"*, which will indicate whether or not the cat or dog actually needs a booster.

Another issue to consider is the size of the vaccine dose given to your cat and hopefully veterinarians are beginning to understand the importance of prescribing vaccine dosage in relation to the actual size of the animal.

For far too long, full doses have traditionally been given to our pets, no matter what their size, when a half dose is sufficient, and giving too much can have a devastating effect on the health of our smaller companions.

Vaccine Shelf Life

Apparently, vaccines which are supposed to be protecting our beloved pets are kept in the refrigerator at the vet's office and lose their potency after a certain period of time (they are dated). Therefore, in order to give them a longer shelf life, the manufacturers make the vaccines 10 times more potent, so they will last longer.

Are you really comfortable with giving your cat a vaccine dose that could be at least 10 times what they actually need, that could be totally unnecessary, and that could result in a tumor or even cause death?

Think about it and educate yourself, because you are the only line of defense between your cat and a healthy life, and it's your choices that will ultimately determine for them how well they live and as your cat's guardian, your first responsibility is their safety.

Bottom line – educate yourself on the vaccines your cat really needs, including the dose and the frequency and find a veterinarian that is willing to listen to common sense.

3. Neutering and Spaying

While it can sometimes be difficult to find the definitive answer when asking when is the best time to neuter or spay your young cat (because there are varying opinions on this topic), one thing that most veterinarians do agree on is that earlier spaying or neutering, between 4 and 6 months of age, is a better choice than waiting.

Spaying or neutering surgeries are carried out under general anesthesia, and as more cats are being neutered at younger ages, speak with your veterinarian and ask for their recommendations regarding the right age to spay or neuter your cat. Following are some points to be aware of:

a) What is Neutering? This surgical procedure is carried out by a licensed veterinarian surgeon to render a male cat unable to reproduce.

In males, the surgery is also referred to as *"castration",* because the procedure involves the removal of the young cat's testicles, leaving behind an empty scrotal sac (which used to contain the kitten's testicles) and this empty sac will soon shrink in size, until it is no longer noticeable.

b) Neutering Males: neutering a male kitten before they are six months of age can help to ensure that they will be less likely to suffer from obesity problems when they grow older.

Neutering can also mean that a male cat will be less likely to have the urge to wander or get into catfights over mating. Furthermore, waiting until a male cat is older than six months before having them neutered could mean that they will experience the effects of raging testosterone that will drive them to spray your furniture or escape their yards by any means necessary to search for females to mate with.

Non-neutered males also tend to spray or mark territory much more often, both inside and outside the home, and during this time they can start to display aggressive tendencies toward other cats as well as people.

c) What is Spaying? This is a surgical procedure (also called *"sterilization")* and is carried out by a licensed veterinarian to prevent the female cat from becoming pregnant and to stop regular heat cycles.

The sterilization procedure is much more involved for a female kitten (than for a male), as it requires the removal of both ovaries and the uterus by incision into the kitten's abdominal cavity. The uterus is also removed during this surgery to prevent the possibility of it becoming infected later on in life.

d) Spaying Females: preferably, a female kitten should be spayed before their very first estrus or heat cycle, which, depending on the particular breed, can be between 4 and 6 months of age.

Females in heat often appear more agitated and irritable while sleeping and eating less and some may become extremely aggressive toward other cats.

Spaying female kittens before their first heat pattern can eliminate these hormonal stressors and reduce the opportunity of mammary glandular tumors. Early spaying may also protect against various other potential concerns, such as uterine infections.

While you may have different ideas about spaying or neutering, perhaps you are unaware that a single pair of cats and their kittens (usually 1-8 per litter) can produce as many as 420,000 kittens in just 7 years. When you realize this, you will probably not want to be part of the problem of over-populated rescues and SPCA facilities, which exist because of the endless suffering of homeless kittens and cats.

Rather, it is unkind and irresponsible not to neuter or spay a cat and beyond not contributing to the overflowing rescue facilities, there are many positive benefits of having this procedure carried out.

e) Effects on Escape and Roaming: a neutered or spayed cat is less likely to wander. Castrated male cats have the tendency to patrol smaller sized outdoor areas and are less likely to participate in territorial conflicts with perceived opponents.

NOTE: a cat that has actually already experienced successful escapes from the yard may continue to wander after they are spayed or neutered.

f) Effects on Problem Elimination: an unsterilized cat may urinate or defecate inside the home or in other undesirable areas in an attempt to stake territorial claims, relieve anxiety, or advertise their available reproductive status.

While neutering or spaying a kitten after they have already begun to inappropriately eliminate or mark territory to announce their sexual availability to other cats will reduce the more powerful urine odor as well as eliminate the hormonal factors, once this habit has begun, the undesirable behavior may continue to persist after neutering or spaying.

g) Possible Weight Gain: while metabolic changes that occur after spaying or neutering can cause some kittens to gain weight, often the real culprit for any weight gain is the human who feels guilty for subjecting their kitten to any kind of pain and therefore attempts to make his or herself feel better by feeding more treats or meals to their feline companion.

If you are concerned about weight gain after neutering or spaying a kitten, simply adjust their food and treat consumption as needed and take time to play with them, so that they receive adequate daily exercise.

It's a very simple process to change your cat's food intake according to their physical demands and how they look, and if your kitten's daily exercise and level of activity has not changed after they have been spayed or neutered, there will likely be no change in food management necessary.

h) Pediatric Spaying/Neutering: in the past, the usual time frame for neutering or spaying a kitten was between the ages of 4 and 6 months.

However, even though there exists quite a bit of debate amongst veterinarians, pediatric spaying or neutering has become more widely accepted.

The American Veterinary Medical Association has supported this concept of very early sterilization since 2004 in an effort to help reduce the numbers of homeless, unwanted animals.

Pediatric spaying or neutering is also called *"prepuberal"* or *"early"* spaying or neutering and may be carried out at a much earlier age, usually between 6 and 14 weeks.

4. Why Vaccinate a Kitten?

Kittens need to be vaccinated by a veterinarian in order to provide them with protection against five common viral diseases referred to as *"FVRCP"*, which stands for Feline Leukemia (FeLV), Rhinotracheitis, Calici and Panoleukopenia and Rabies.

Approximately one week after your kitten has completed all three sets of primary vaccinations, they will be fully protected from those specific diseases.

While most veterinarians will recommend a once a year vaccination for the next year or two, think seriously about this because all they may need is a blood test to test for circulating antibodies.

If your veterinarian is insisting on a yearly vaccination for your cat, you need to ask them why, because this would be considered by most professionals to be *"over vaccinating"*. Whether or not your cat actually needs a booster can be determined with a simple blood test.

5. Common Diseases and Viruses

Cats are commonly vaccinated against the following diseases and viruses, referred to as *"FVRCP"*:

1) Feline Calici (FCV): there are several different strains of the highly contagious and easily transmitted calici virus, and much like the human flu, this virus is able to mutate and develop new strains and symptoms varying from loss of appetite, associated with upper respiratory infections (URI) or "colds", pneumonia, limping and death.

This virus can be transmitted through the air when a cat sneezes, from a shared water dish or litter box, or from direct contact with an infected cat.

2) Feline Leukemia (FeLV): while this virus is the leading cause of death in cats (next to trauma), killing 85% of infected felines within three years of being diagnosed, it doesn't have to be a death sentence, because it can be prevented through vaccination.

This virus (that suppresses the immune system) is a disease that only affects cats, which means that it cannot be transmitted to other animals or people. While the virus does not live more than a few hours when outside the cat's body, it can be passed from one cat to another through blood, saliva, urine and feces, causing anemia or lymphoma (cancer of the lymph nodes, spleen, thymus, bone marrow and other parts of the body).

The most common way for this infection to spread is when cats are fighting with one another and kittens can become infected in the uterus or through mother's milk by an otherwise healthy appearing cat.

3) Panleukopenia (FPV - feline distemper): this highly contagious and often fatal (especially in young kittens or cats) viral disease, for which there is no cure, is often called feline distemper and while preventable through vaccination, has a very high mortality rate.

This virus is spread through an infected cat's blood, feces, nasal discharge, saliva or urine and cats of all ages can become infected, with symptoms causing severe gastrointestinal problems including vomiting, diarrhea, bloody stool, weight loss and weakness.

Once diagnosed, and with aggressive treatment that may include hospitalization to administer antibiotics, intravenous therapy, medication to suppress vomiting and diarrhea and proper nutritional support, the infected cat may survive.

4) Rhinotracheitis (FHV-1 - Feline Herpesvirus): this virus, which is species specific (meaning that it only can infect cats of all ages) is a major cause of upper respiratory infections. FHV-1 is also a common cause of conjunctivitis, which is inflammation of the eye tissues.

The virus is excreted through saliva, or nose and eye secretions from an infected cat and another cat can be infected by coming into contact with these secretions or an inanimate object that the cat may have sneezed or drooled upon.

While there is no cure for a cat that may be infected with a herpes virus infection, and the vaccine will not completely prevent an infection if your cat is exposed to the virus, most cats respond well to management of the condition and can lead normal lives.

Treatment will involve vaccination, antibiotics to prevent secondary infections, L-Lysine supplementation to reduce viral relapse, saline drops for the eyes and salmon oil added to the cat's food to make it smell more palatable so they will eat it.

5) Rabies: is a viral disease transmitted by coming into contact with the saliva of an infected animal, usually through a bite. The virus travels to the brain along the nerves and once symptoms develop, death is almost certainly inevitable, usually following a prolonged period of suffering.

If you plan to travel out of State or across country borders, you will need to make sure that your cat has an up to date Rabies Vaccination Certificate indicating they have been inoculated against rabies.

Vaccinating cats against rabies is also compulsory in most countries in mainland Europe, as is permanent identification and registration of cats through the use of a Pet Passport.

Those living in a country that is rabies free (UK, Eire) are not required to vaccinate their cats against rabies, unless they intend to travel.

6. When Is a Kitten Vaccinated?

While the antibodies in the mother's milk protect young kittens from infection, after they are starting to eat solid food at around six weeks of age, most veterinarians will advise that it's time to have them vaccinated against the five common *"FVRCP"* viral diseases (noted above).

Depending on the vaccination schedule of the particular breeder, the kitten may have received their first combination vaccination needle around six to eight weeks of age, before their new guardian takes them home.

Generally speaking, kitten vaccinations will be given at 3 to 4-week intervals until the cat is 16-20 weeks (4 to 4 ½ months) old and maternal antibody is out of the system. For adult cats with an unknown vaccination history, the vaccine series will usually consist of two doses of vaccine, 3 to 4 weeks apart.

You will want to educate yourself and talk openly with your chosen veterinarian with respect to how vaccines work, the many pros and cons, whether your cat needs them, whether the benefits outweigh the risks, and how much and how often because it is known that vaccines may cause unwanted adverse effects.

Hopefully, you will take the time to choose a veterinarian that is more interested in keeping up to date with current research and vaccine guidelines and recommendations based on current evidence, rather than on their monthly billing and what was thought to be appropriate in the past.

7. Worms, Worms & More Worms

How can a cat get worms, you might ask. Depending on the cat's lifestyle (indoor or outdoor), while there may be several different ways a cat can develop a case of worms, this usually happens when the cat comes into contact with eggs or infected particles in feces. For instance, this can happen in a litter box when they step in the feces, because then they ingest them during their grooming process.

An outdoor cat may be hunting mice or rats that already have the worm larvae and when they bite, kill or ingest any of the infected tissue, then the worms can take up residence and grow in the cat's intestines.

Also, young kittens that are nursing from an infected mother can develop a roundworm infestation, which is often noticeable if the kitten has a very bloated abdomen.

The two most common types of worms that may infest your companion are roundworms and tapeworms, both of which can be passed on to humans, and (thankfully) the de-worming process is fairly simple and will effectively kill these internal parasites.

It is also possible for your cat or kitten to be infested with hookworms and whipworms.

A microscopic stool examination will reveal the type of worms and medications will be given by mouth with a follow-up stool exam to ensure the parasite has been eliminated.

A typical regimen for eliminating roundworms (for example) might involve giving medication once a day for three days, with repeated dosing three weeks later and possibly once again three months later. Many veterinarians recommend worming cats for tapeworm and roundworms every 6-12 months.

The health risks to your kitten or cat include diarrhea, vomiting, slow growth, and in serious cases a bowel blockage, pneumonia, even death.

Most kittens and cats will experience worms at some stage in their life and thankfully the problem can be easily and swiftly eliminated with worming medication.

8. Other Diseases and Viruses

Of course, there are many other diseases and viruses that may or may not affect your cat during his or her lifetime, such as:

1) Feline Immunodeficiency Virus (FIV): this common virus, which affects the worldwide cat population, is sometimes referred to as feline AIDS, because it launches a widespread attack on the cat's immune system.

While illness and death can arise from a wide variety of secondary infections that the cat's body cannot fight off, the infected cat may not show signs until years after they have been initially infected. Causing problems in the digestive tract, tell tale signs of this virus are usually diarrhea and vomiting.

2) Bordetella and Mycoplasma: these viruses attack the cat's lower airways (trachea and lungs). An infected cat may have trouble breathing or may have a raspy sound to his or her meow.

3) Feline Infectious Peritonitis (FIP): this is one of the slow acting feline virus diseases. It can cause inflammation in several different organs. It can result in serious illness and death.

4) Parvovirus: is the most common virus that causes problems in the cat's digestive tract. Diarrhea and vomiting are tell-tale clinical signs.

5) Heartworm: this infectious health problem, that is spread by infected mosquitoes, can cause lung disease in cats with the resulting immune reaction being the cause of severe health problems.

6) High-Rise Syndrome: while you might think that this name refers to cats that are afraid of heights, you'd be wrong, because it actually refers to the high incidence of cats falling or jumping from open windows that results in broken legs, jaws and pelvis, punctured lungs and often death.

7) Ringworm (dermatophytosis): not actually a worm, this is a highly contagious viral fungus that can infect the skin, hair and nails of cats, other pets and humans and it is called "ringworm" because it causes patchy, circular areas of hair loss with central red rings.

8) Diabetes: is a complex disease caused by either a lack of, or inadequate response to insulin. Similar to what happens to humans, when a cat eats, the digestive system breaks down the food into various components and when the body is not able to produce or utilize insulin efficiently, the result is elevated blood sugar levels and hyperglycemia. Many complicated health problems may arise, if this is left untreated.

9) Cancer: there are many forms of cancer than can afflict a cat, which may be localized in the form of a tumor, or can spread throughout the cat's entire body.

10) Eye Infections: bacteria, chemicals, fungi, parasites and viruses are often common causes for eye infections in cats with the usual symptoms presenting as redness, swelling and discharge and your cat squinting and rubbing at their eyes and often with nasal discharge and sneezing.

Treatment will depend on discovering the underlying cause and mild occurrences will often resolve with rest, good hydration and nutrition, while more severe cases may require the application of topical ointments or medications to eliminate the microbe causing the infection.

Keep in mind that many of the microbes that cause infection are highly contagious to other felines, and some can also be transmitted to humans, such as the Bartonella bacteria and Toxoplasma parasites.

11) Corneal Ulcers: are characterized by open sores and loss of tissue from the surface of the eye and may be the result of anatomical abnormality or inadequate tear production, infection or injury.

You may notice redness, discharge and your cat squinting or appearing to be in pain and the ulcer may present as a cloudy area on the cat's cornea. The good news is that with proper treatment, a superficial ulcer will often heal, while deeper ulcers may require surgery or if the trauma is severe, the ulcer may rupture and cause blindness.

12) Eye Trauma: is a relatively common cause of eye problems in cats, especially those who wander about in the great outdoors where they can easily encounter foreign materials, thorny bushes and other cats who may challenge them to a fight that may result in scratches or puncture wounds to the surface of the eye.

If they suffer a severe blow to the head (if it doesn't kill them), they can suffer from *"Proptosis"*, which is the medical term describing an eye that has become dislodged from the socket.

There may be many symptoms of eye trauma, ranging from drainage, swelling and redness to visible damage with the resulting treatment ranging from antibiotic drops or ointments to surgery.

13) Eye Allergies: generally speaking, cats have sensitive eyes that can easily become irritated, itchy and watery from dust, fragrances, cleaning chemicals, tobacco or other smoke and more. If the problem is mild, a simple eye wash solution may be all that is required to relieve the problem, if you can get your cat to hold still long enough for you to perform this task.

14) Iris Melanosis: the iris is the colored area of your cat's eyes and other than when they have those blue kitten eyes that change to adult color as they mature, a cat's eye color will remain the same during adulthood.

However, the development of brown *"freckles"* or patches of different colored pigment can occur on the iris of a middle-aged or older cat. While this *"Melanosis"* does not usually cause any problems, in a severe case it may cause dysfunction of the iris, which can then lead to glaucoma.

You will want to be careful not to confuse this type of iris Melanosis with the similar sounding *"Iris Melanoma",* which can be a serious type of cancer. Therefore, any new dark pigment appearing on your cat's iris should be reported to your veterinarian.

15) Glaucoma (increased eye pressure): in a healthy eye, fluid is always being produced inside and drained from within the eyeball and if the drainage becomes blocked, eye pressure will increase, which will then result in painful glaucoma.

This may have been caused by many different reasons from trauma to infection, producing red, draining and in serious cases, enlarged eyes, which will require emergency attention because the cat can suffer a loss of eyesight or even lose their eyes if underlying causes are not identified and they do not receive medication to reduce the pressure.

16) Cataracts: in common with aging humans, our cats also can develop cataracts, when the usually clear lens develops a cloudy cataract that prevents light from reaching the back of the eye.

Depending on the severity of the cataract, this can result in poor or reduced vision or total blindness. While cataract surgery is now available for cats, if the cost of having this performed is prohibitive, keep in mind that most indoor cats can adapt amazingly well to having poor vision.

17) Obesity: just like there is an obesity epidemic in the human world, the same is true of our fur friends who are suffering from obesity in increasingly large numbers.

Why are there so many fat cats? The most obvious answer is not what you might think because while most humans might believe that a cat is fat simply because his or her guardian is over-feeding them, the real reason is most likely because we humans are feeding them the wrong food.

Carnivores are designed to meet their energy needs with calories supplied by protein and fat – not by carbohydrates, and yet we humans are feeding our cats a dry kibble diet that usually ranges from 35% – 50% carbs.

This usually means that our kibble fed cats are receiving 5 to 10 times more carbs than what they would naturally eat in the wild, because it's convenient for us humans and doesn't require any special storage care.

This is a serious disconnect between what the cat is designed to eat and what we humans insist on feeding and it is simple math, because cats use a minimal amount of carbohydrates for energy and what is not used is stored as fat.

The bottom line is that feeding your cat the least expensive canned cat food is still a better option for their health than feeding them the most expensive dry kibble diet, because at least with the canned food they are getting some very essential moisture in their meal.

Free Feeding: another important factor that contributes to obesity in our cats is the free feeding that most of us have been brainwashed to believe is the proper way to feed a cat. This means that our cats (that are supposed to self-regulate their food intake) are provided with a never-ending supply of kibble, that they can choose to eat whenever the mood strikes them.

While free feeding may be alright for cats that are able to self-regulate their food intake, some cats have no off switch and will regularly overeat, often because the sneaky food manufacturers coat the kibble with enticing animal protein, which is highly appealing to the average cat and is designed to entice them to eat more of this high carb food.

Further, some cats tend to overeat when given dry food because they are designed to be satiated after ingesting an appropriate amount of fat and protein and since there is such a small percentage found in dry kibble, they have to eat more of it before their brain signals *"I'm full"*.

Finally, some cats eat too much throughout their free feeding day because they are bored, and as you can imagine, this is especially true for cats that spend their entire lives indoors as there is much less to keep their minds occupied and they generally burn fewer calories that an outdoor cat because of their lower activity level.

18) Tick Born Diseases: while most ticks don't carry disease and most cats live their entire lives never acquiring a tick-related illness (which may be because cats are much more hypersensitive to changes in their environment and on their bodies than our canine friends) and will remove a tick before it has a chance to attach itself), tick born diseases are sometimes seen by vets, including:

a) Bobcat Fever (Feline Cytauxzoonosis): this blood and tissue infection is the result of the *"Cytauxzoon felis"* blood parasite that manifests itself, causing hemorrhage and death to its host in approximately three weeks from the time of infection.

The reason this infection is known as "Bobcat Fever" is because while the bobcat is the natural host or carrier of this disease, they are not affected by it. Rather, the Lone Star ticks feed on the blood of the bobcat until the ticks drop off their body as part of the process of their next life stage, and when these ticks attach to a domesticated cat that is not immune to the disease, they can be infected.

The only good thing about this disease is that it can only be passed on by a tick that has fed on the bobcat's blood, which means that becoming infected would be quite rare, unless your cat is allowed to roam freely outdoors and lives in close proximity to a bobcat habitat (which in most cases would be in the southeast and Midwestern United States).

If your cat does become infected, prognosis for recovery is not good and they will suffer from breathing difficulties, loss of appetite, dehydration, high fever, depression, anemia and jaundice, which usually will lead to death, and even those that do pull through may still suffer from a recurrence.

b) Rabbit Fever (Tularemia): is usually a fatal disease, carried by the American Dog tick, the Lone Star tick, the Pacific Coast tick and the Rocky Mountain wood tick and is caused by the bacteria *"Francisella tularensis"*.

First, the ticks become infected when they feed on animals or birds that are infected, and then when a cat (for instance) is bitten by the tick any time during the tick's two-year cycle or the cat eats an infected rabbit, bird or other creature, they become infected.

The Tularemia infection can range in severity from mild swelling of lymph nodes, ulcers in the mouth and fever to death, with multiple symptoms such as high fever, enlarged lymph nodes, abscess at the area of the tick bite, eye and nose discharge, tiredness, and liver or spleen abscesses.

While Tularemia can be diagnosed with a blood test, most often it's not diagnosed until after a cat dies from it. It's important to know that Tularemia is a zoonotic disease, which means that it can be transmitted to humans if they receive a scratch or a bite from a cat that is already infected.

c) Haemobartonellosis: this mouthful of a potentially deadly tick-borne disease is also known as *"feline infectious anemia"* or *"feline hemotropic mycoplasmosis"*. This is an illness that attacks the red blood cells that carry oxygen throughout the body and is more commonly seen than either Bobcat or Rabbit Fever.

This type of anemia belongs to a group of microorganisms called *"mycoplasma"* that live inside the cat's red blood cells and it is transferred to the cat by infected ticks and fleas that feed on the cat.

The mycoplasma can also be passed to another animal or human through an infected blood transfusion or through cat bites and the mother cat can infect their kittens through the placenta.

Symptoms can range in severity from very mild (involving a slight anemia), to severe, including loss of appetite, weight loss, dehydration, accelerated heart rate and respiration, depression, white gums, weakness and sudden death.

Once diagnosed, cats will be given antibiotics for a three-week period, and cats with more severely progressed symptoms may require hospitalization and blood transfusion.

NOTE: although similar sounding, the haemobartonellosis disease is an entirely different disease from *"feline bartonellosis"*, which is an infectious bacterial disease commonly known as *"Cat Scratch Fever"*.

d) Babesiosis: this parasitic disease is another rare tick-borne disease in cats, caused by the *"Babesia felis"* parasite. While infections take hold approximately two weeks after exposure and are believed to occur most often through tick bites, the parasite can also be transferred via blood transfer from a bite or scratch, blood transfusions, or through the placenta in pregnant cats.

Symptoms can include lack of appetite, weight loss, low energy, anemia and jaundice. If symptoms remain mild in an infected cat, it may be months or even years before this disease is diagnosed, and depending on the severity of the disease, treatment may include malarial drugs, antibiotics, blood transfusions (for severe anemia) and supportive care.

If your cat is permitted to roam about outdoors and is spending time in an area that is a known tick habitat, always check your cat daily for the presence of ticks and promptly remove any that are found, because the longer a tick stays on the body, the more likely the parasite will be transferred.

e) Ehrlichiosis: this tick-borne disease is transmitted by both the Brown Dog Tick and the Lone Star Tick and has been reported in every State in the US, as well as worldwide. Common symptoms include depression, reduced appetite, fever, stiff and painful joints and bruising.

Signs of infection typically occur less than a month after a tick bite and last for approximately four weeks and there is no vaccine available. Blood tests may be required to test for antibodies and treatment will require a course of antibiotics for up to four weeks, in order to completely clear the organism from the infected cat's system.

After a cat has been previously infected, they may develop antibodies to the organism, but will not be immune to being re-infected. Cats permitted outside that live in areas of the country where the Ehrlichiosis tick disease is common or widespread, may be prescribed low doses of antibiotics during tick season.

f) Feline Bartonellosis: this infectious, zoonotic, bacterial disease is caused by the *"Bartonella henselae"* bacteria and is commonly called "Cat Scratch Disease" or "Cat Scratch Fever", because it can be passed on to other animals and humans when they are scratched or licked by a cat that has been infected.

Infected fleas leave their feces on the cat's skin and when the cat cleans their fur, they ingest the feces containing the bacteria and become infected themselves. While the cat will not suffer severely from this infection, if the cat bites, licks or scratches another animal or a human, the fever can be passed on.

While infection of this bacterium is usually mild in humans and not fatal, it is estimated that each year over 12,000 people are diagnosed with cat scratch disease in the United States, with many of the infected being children who are most likely to play with kittens that often bite and scratch during play.

Those infected may experience swelling of the lymph nodes, headache, fever and a feeling of tiredness and while some patients may require antibiotics, most will usually resolve on themselves with no medical intervention.

NOTE: while Cat Scratch Fever is not fatal for humans, it can still be a considerable risk to those who may already have a compromised immune system.

9. Special Care When Pregnant

A female cat can attain sexual maturity between five and six months of age, and feline pregnancy lasts approximately 61 to 72 days. The mother (the *"queen"*) will usually produce between 4 and 6 kittens per litter and can produce two litters every year.

Immediately upon noticing signs of pregnancy, you will want to take your cat to your veterinarian to confirm the pregnancy and to receive instructions for the proper feeding and care.

During the first couple of weeks of pregnancy your queen may experience morning sickness. Your veterinarian may recommend increasing food intake or adding an egg or cottage cheese to your cat's meals and switching to kitten kibble (which is higher in protein) at around the 30-day mark.

As the female becomes heavier with the kittens, she will often lose interest in exercising and she will need to sleep more.

When the time for birthing is drawing near (about a week before), the female will start to display "nesting" characteristics where she will search for a warm and safe place to give birth.

You can help by providing a nesting box and she will likely want to take things into the box to make it more comfortable, such as towels or even a stuffed toy that she will begin to mother. When the time draws closer to birthing (about two days before), the female may completely lose her appetite and show signs of distress by pacing and acting uncomfortable.

Once the mother gives birth to her first kitten, the remaining kittens should arrive approximately every 15 to 20 minutes, until the last one has been born. The mother will usually clean up the kittens by licking them and eating the placentas that provide her with the extra nutrition she needs.

10. Pet Insurance

Pet guardians commonly ask themselves, when considering medical insurance for their cat, whether they can afford <u>not</u> to have it.

On the one hand, in light of all the new treatments and medications that are now available for our fur friends that usually come with a very high price tag, an increasing number of guardians have decided to add pet insurance to their list of monthly expenses.

On the other hand, some humans believe that placing money into a savings account, in case unforeseen medical treatments are required, makes more sense.

Pet insurance coverage can cost anywhere from $2,000 to $6,000 (£1,201 to £3,604) over an average lifespan of a cat, and unless your cat is involved in a serious accident or contracts a life-threatening disease, you may never need to pay out that much for treatment.

Whether you decide to start a savings account for your cat so that you will always have funds available for unforeseen health issues or you decide to buy a health insurance plan, most cat lovers will go to any lengths to save the life of their beloved companions.

However, even in the face of rapidly increasing costs of caring for our cats, owners purchasing pet insurance remain a small minority.

Even though you might believe that pet insurance will be your savior anytime your cat requires a trip to the vet's office, you really need to be careful when considering an insurance plan, because there are many policies that contain small print excluding certain ages or chronic conditions.

Unfortunately, most people don't consider pet insurance when their pets are healthy because buying pet insurance means playing the odds, and unless your cat becomes seriously ill, you end up paying for something that might never happen.

However, (just like car insurance) you can't buy it after you've had that accident and the older your cat, the higher the premiums.

In other words, if you're planning on purchasing health insurance for your cat, do it before any problems arise in order to avoid having conditions that may present themselves in the future from being excluded from your policy.

As well, you need to keep in mind that feline health insurance rates will likely increase as your cat gets older. When your cat is younger your policy may only be $17 (£12) per month, but it may increase considerably to as much as $170 (£121) or more per month as your cat becomes middle or senior aged (at around 7 years of age).

Since many of us in today's uncertain economy may be hard pressed to pay a high veterinarian bill, generally speaking, the alternative of paying monthly pet insurance premiums will provide peace of mind and improved veterinarian care for our best friends.

Shop around, because (as with all insurance policies) pet insurance policies will vary greatly between companies and the only way to know for certain exactly what sort of coverage you are buying is to closely exam the policy, read and understand what will and what will not be covered.

There are several considerations to be aware of before choosing to purchase a pet insurance policy, including:

- Is your cat required to undergo a physical exam?
- Is there a waiting period before the policy becomes active?
- What percentage of the bill does the insurance company pay?
- Are payments limited or capped in any way?
- Are there co-pays (cost to you upfront)?
- Does the plan cover pre-existing conditions?
- Does the plan cover chronic or recurring medical problems?
- Can you choose any vet or animal hospital to treat your pet?
- Are prescription medications covered?
- Are you covered when traveling with your pet?
- Does the policy pay if your pet is being treated and then dies?

When you love your cat and worry that you may not have the funds to cover an emergency medical situation that could unexpectedly cost thousands, the right pet insurance policy will provide both peace of mind and better health care for your beloved fur friend.

11. Identifying and Finding Lost Cats

a) Micro-Chipping: this implant is a very small integrated circuit, approximately twice the size of a grain of rice, enclosed in glass that is implanted underneath the cat's skin (or other animal) with a syringe.

The chip uses passive Radio Frequency Identification (RFID) technology and is also known as a PIT tag (Passive Integrated Transponder).

The microchip is usually implanted without anaesthetic into the scruff of a cat's neck by a veterinarian or shelter and has no internal power source, which means that they must be read by a scanner or *"interrogator"* that energizes the capacitor in the chip, which then sends radio signals back to the scanner so that the identifying number can be read.

Manufacturers of microchips often donate scanners to animal shelters and veterinarian clinics and hospitals.

While many communities are proposing making micro-chipping of all cats mandatory and micro-chipping is a requirements for any cats traveling to the state of Hawaii, many others are not especially pleased with this idea because they believe it's just more big business for little reward.

While it has become the law in many countries to microchip dogs, micro-chipping cats is still at the discretion of their guardians.

Even though micro-chipping is used by animal shelters, pounds, animal control officers, breeders and veterinarians in order to help return a higher percentage of lost cats to their owners, some of the resistance to this idea can be explained by inherent problems with the ability of some organizations to correctly read the implants.

As an example, if the scanner is not tuned to the same frequency as the implanted microchip, it will not be read which renders the process useless.

Pet microchips are manufactured with different frequencies, including 125 kHz, 128 kHz and 134.2 kHz. While approximately 98% of the pet microchips in the US use 125 kHz, those in Europe use 134.2 kHz.

In other words, if the facility reading your cat's microchip does not have a compatible scanner, your cat will not be identified and returned to you.

Further, what may turn out to be worse than the scanner incompatibility problem could be increasing evidence to indicate that microchips might cause Cancer.

As well, some microchips will migrate inside the cat's body and while they may start out in the cat's neck, they could end up in their leg or some other body part.

You will have to weigh information known about microchips (including possible Cancer risks) and the odds of losing your cat to decide whether or not a microchip is something you want to have for your cat.

Whether or not you choose a microchip for your cat, generally the cost will be around $45 (£32) depending on what your veterinarian may charge for this service.

b) Tattooing: cats are tattooed to help identify them in case they are lost or stolen. Many cat guardians prefer this safe, simple solution to micro-chipping, because there is no need to locate a scanner that reads the correct frequency and there are no known side effects.

Because a tattoo is visible (usually on the inside of the ear), it is immediately recognizable and reported when a lost cat is found, which means that tattooing could easily be the most effective means of identification available.

As well, cat thieves may be less likely to steal a cat that has a permanent visible form of identification.

The largest international registry (Tattoo-A-Pet) has a 24-hour lost pet hotline and the fee for tattooing and registering a cat for their lifetime is approximately $40 (£29).

c) Pet Trackers: in today's electronic world, many people are wondering if a Pet Tracker might be a good idea for helping to keep their beloved feline safe. So, what exactly are Pet Trackers, how much do they cost, how do they work and how do you know which one to choose?

First of all, you need to know that there are many in the marketplace and that there are basically two categories comprised of: (1) Cellular

GPS Trackers and (2) Radio Trackers, which are a special collar attached to your cat.

A GPS Tracker can help you locate your cat in real time by utilizing cellular towers and requires the use of a SIM card or some sort of cellular service, with average pricing ranging from $100 (£71) to $300 (£214).

Radio Trackers (which have been used for decades) utilize what some may consider outdated technology, functioning over a limited range, much like a "Walkie Talkie". The more you spend for a Radio Tracker, the greater the range will be and pricing can range from $200 (£143) to $1,000 (£713).

d) Where to Look: if your cat goes missing, there are many places you can contact and steps you can take that may help you locate your lost cat, including:

- Retracing your cat's last known location
- Contacting your friends and neighbors
- Putting up flyers on telephone poles throughout your neighborhood with your contact details and your cat's photo
- Calling all local shelters and pounds every day
- Contacting local rescue organizations
- Contacting local schools - children might have seen your cat
- Distributing flyers with a photograph of your cat and your contact details in all neighborhood stores and businesses
- Contacting all businesses that deal with lost pets
- Posting a picture on Facebook or other social media
- Asking your local radio station for help
- Advertising in your local newspaper

12. Yearly Cost of Ownership

It can be difficult to accurately estimate what the cost of owning every cat might be because there are too many variables, not to mention unexpected medical problems that may not otherwise be considered average.

For instance, you may like to buy the latest toys, beds, viewing towers or gadgets or the most expensive food for your cat every week that might also not be considered average. However, when thinking about sharing your life with a Scottish Fold cat, it's important to consider more than just the daily cost of feeding.

Many humans do not think about whether or not they can truly afford to care for a cat before they bring one home, and not being prepared can cause stress and problems later on.

Remember that being financially responsible for your cat is a large part of being a good guardian. Beyond the initial investment of purchasing your kitten from a reputable breeder, for most guardians owning a Scottish Fold will include the costs associated with the following:

- Food and Treats
- Litter box, Litter
- Collars, Leashes
- Travel kennels
- Toys
- Beds
- Professional Grooming or Equipment
- Shampoo and Conditioner
- Neutering or Spaying
- Regular Veterinary Care
- Pet Sitting or Boarding
- Pet Insurance
- Tattooing or Micro-chipping
- Unexpected Emergencies

As you can see from the list above, there are many variables involved in being a feline guardian that may or may not apply to your particular situation.

For instance, depending upon where you shop, what type of food and how much you feed your cat, what sort of veterinarian or grooming care you choose, whether or not you have pet insurance and what types of items you purchase for your cat's well-being, the yearly cost of owning a Scottish Fold could be estimated at $1,000 (£713) or more for the first year and anywhere between $500 and $700 (£357 and £499) or more each year thereafter, plus any emergency expenses.

Other contributing factors that may have an effect on the initial cost and overall yearly cost of owning a cat can include the pedigree of your cat, the breeder's expertise, the breed popularity, the region where you live, the accessibility of the items you need, your own lifestyle preferences and your cat's age and individual needs.

NOTE: the more popular, trendy or unusual a particular breed may be, the more significant expertise and experience of the breeder, and the more positive traits that breed may enjoy, could also make the cost of initially purchasing a kitten from a breeder more costly.

Chapter 14: Cat Grooming

You will want to get your kitten used to the routine of simple grooming early on, so that they will not be traumatized for the rest of their life every time grooming is necessary.

Not taking the time to regularly involve your kitten in grooming sessions could lead to serious, unwanted behavior that may include trauma to your cat, not to mention stress or injury to yourself in the form of biting and scratching (that could result in a lifetime of unhappy grooming sessions).

When you neglect regular, daily or at least a weekly home grooming session with your kitten or cat to remove dead hair and check toenails, this will not only cost you and your feline companion in terms of possible trauma, but it may also cost you in veterinarian fees should you not be aware of a problem that could have been discovered early on during regular grooming sessions.

An effective home regimen should include not just surface brushing, but also getting to all those sensitive areas easily missed around the ears and collar area, the armpit area, and the back end and tail.

Do not allow yourself to get caught in the *"my cat doesn't like it"* trap, which is an excuse many owners will use to avoid regular grooming sessions.

When you allow your cat to dictate whether they will permit a grooming session, you are setting a dangerous precedent that could lead to a lifetime of trauma for both you and your cat.

When humans neglect daily grooming routines, many cats develop a heightened sensitivity, especially with regard to having their legs and feet held, their ears inspected or their nails clipped, and will do anything they can to avoid the process when you need to groom them.

Make a pact with yourself right from the first day you bring your kitten home never to neglect a regular grooming routine, such as regular brushing, trimming toenails or brushing teeth, just because your cat may not particularly *"like"* it.

Remember that a few minutes of regular grooming sessions each day with your Scottish Fold is also a wonderful opportunity for bonding and when you have the right tools, it can be a pleasurable experience for you both.

For instance, a company called *"Amazingly Cat"* has a "gentle de-shedding glove" that easily removes all that excess dead cat fur, which cuts down on the hair-covered furniture and clothing. This looks like a winner for both cat and human, as all you do is pet your cat while wearing the glove.

1. Occasionally a Bath

Sometimes, even a cat needs a bath, so make sure you have all the proper shampoos and conditioners on hand, including a flea shampoo just in case.

Step One: before you get your cat or kitten anywhere near the water, it's important to make sure that you brush out any debris, dead hair, mats or tangles from their coat prior to beginning the bathing process.

As well, removing any debris or mats from your cat's coat beforehand will make the entire process easier on both you, your cat and your drains (which will become clogged with dead hair if you don't remove it beforehand).

Step Two: first lay down a rubber bath mat to provide a more secure footing for your cat and to prevent your sink from being scratched.

Step Three: have everything you need for the bath (shampoo, conditioner, sponge, towels) right next to the tub or in the shower, so you don't have to go searching once your cat is already wet.

Step Four: place balls in your cat's ear canals to prevent accidental splashes from entering the ear canal that could later cause an ear infection.

Step Five: fill your sink or tub with four to six inches (10 to 15 cm) of lukewarm water (not too hot as cats are more sensitive to hot water than us humans) and put your Scottish Fold in the water. Completely wet your cat's coat right down to the skin by using a detachable showerhead. If you don't have a spray attachment, a cup or pitcher will work just as well.

No cat likes to have water poured over its head and into its eyes, so use a wet sponge or wash cloth to wet the head area.

Step Six: apply shampoo as indicated on the bottle instructions by beginning at the head and working your way down the back. Be careful not to get shampoo in the eyes, nose, mouth or ears. Comb the shampoo lather through your cat's hair with your fingers, making sure you don't miss the areas under the legs and tail.

Step Seven: after allowing the shampoo to remain in your cat's coat for a couple of minutes, thoroughly rinse the coat right down to the skin with clean, lukewarm water using the spray attachment, cup or pitcher. Comb through your cat's coat with your fingers to make sure all shampoo residue has been completely rinsed away.

Any shampoo remaining in a cat's coat will lead to irritation and itching. Once you've rinsed, take the time to rinse again, especially in the armpits and underneath the tail area. Use your hands to gently squeeze all excess water from your cat's coat.

Step Eight: apply conditioner as indicated on the bottle instructions and work the conditioner throughout your cat's coat. Leave the conditioner in your cat's coat for two minutes and then thoroughly rinse again with warm water, unless the conditioner you are using is a *"leave-in"*, no-rinse formula.

It is also a good idea to choose a brand of conditioner that contains sunscreen to help protect from ultraviolet radiation when your cat is outside on sunny days.

Applying a good conditioner containing protein to your cat's coat after bathing will help to rebuild, restructure and protect the coat by bonding to the shaft of each individual hair.

Pull the plug on your tub and let the water drain away as you use your hands to squeeze excess water from your cat's legs and feet.

Step Nine: immediately out of the water, wrap your cat in dry towels so they don't get cold and use the towels to gently squeeze out extra water before you allow them to shake and spray water everywhere. Unless it's a warm day out, you will want to carefully dry your cat or kitten right away with your handheld hairdryer.

Use your hand or a soft brush or comb to lift and fluff the coat to help it dry more quickly. You will want to place your hand between the hairdryer and your cat's hair so that they will never get a direct blast of hot air and never blow air directly into their face or ears.

Don't forget to remove the cotton balls from his or her ears and make sure the ears are dry.

2. Ear Care

There are many ear cleaning creams, drops, oils, rinses, solutions and wipes formulated for cleaning your cat's ears that you can purchase from your local pet store or veterinarian's office.

Alternatively, you may prefer to use a home remedy that will just as efficiently clean your cat's ears, such as Witch Hazel or a 50:50 mixture of hydrogen peroxide and purified water.

If you are going to make your own ear-cleaning solution, find a bottle with a nozzle, measure your solution, put it properly diluted and mixed into the bottle and use your preparation to saturate a cotton makeup remover pad to wipe out the visible part of your cat's ears. Always make sure the ears are totally dried after cleaning.

3. Eye Care

Every cat should have their eyes gently wiped with a warm, damp cloth to remove any build-up of daily secretions in the corners of the eyes that can be unattractive and uncomfortable for the cat (and could also become a cause of bacterial yeast growth that can lead to eye infections).

When you take a moment every day to gently wipe your cat's eyes with a warm and moist cloth, you will help to keep your cat's eyes comfortable and infection free.

4. Nail Care

Allowing your cat to have long, untrimmed nails can result in various health hazards, including infections or an irregular and uncomfortable gait that can result in damage to their skeleton. Also, cats with really long nails can get their claws caught in soft material, such as carpets, clothing or furniture.

Although most cats do not particularly enjoy the process of having their nails trimmed (and most humans find the exercise to be a little scary), regular nail trimming is a very important grooming practice that should never be overlooked.

When you get them used to having their nails trimmed at a young age, they will quietly tolerate the process for the rest of their life. In order to keep your adult cat's toenails in good condition and the proper length, you will need to purchase a pair of nail scissors at a pet store and learn how to correctly use them.

Generally speaking, when you gently squeeze your cat's paws, this causes the nails to protrude or unsheathe and then you can clearly see if the nails are too long.

If there is a long curve at the end, all you need to do is snip off the curved tip of each nail with your nail scissors.

It's not necessary to trim the nails really short and you need to be aware that cutting into the pink nail quick will cause pain to your cat and the nails will bleed.

After snipping the curved tips, your cat will likely want to sharpen their claws on a convenient scratching post, and if you don't buy one for your cat and teach them how to use it, they may decide to use the convenient arm of your favorite couch, instead.

5. Dental Care

As a conscientious cat guardian, you will need to regularly care for your cat's teeth throughout their entire life.

a) Primary Teeth: often a young kitten will not naturally lose their kitten or baby teeth until they are at least 6 to 7 months of age.

If your kitten has not naturally lost all their baby teeth, any remaining teeth will need to be pulled in order to allow room for the adult teeth to properly grow in, and the best time to do this will be the same time as they visit the veterinarian's office to be spayed or neutered.

b) Periodontal Disease: please be aware that 85% of four-year-old cats suffer from some form of periodontal disease and bad breath, because their guardians do <u>not</u> look after their cat's teeth.

What makes this shocking statistic even worse is that with simple, daily care it is possible to entirely prevent feline gum disease and bad breath.

The pain associated with periodontal disease will make your cat's life miserable, as it will be painful for them to eat and the associated bacteria can infect many parts of the cat's body, including the heart, kidney, liver and brain, all of which they will have to suffer in silence.

If your cat has bad breath, this could be the first sign of an unhealthy mouth and gum disease caused by plaque build-up on the teeth.

As well, if your cat is drooling excessively, this may be a symptom secondary to dental disease, because your cat may be experiencing pain or the salivary glands may be reacting to inflammation from excessive bacteria in the mouth.

If you notice your cat drooling and it's not because they're anticipating a tasty dinner you are about to serve them, you will want to have your cat professionally examined at your veterinarian's office.

c) Teeth Brushing: slowly introduce your cat to teeth brushing early on in their young life, so that they will not fear it.

Begin with a finger cap toothbrush when they are young kittens and then move to a soft bristled toothbrush or even an electric brush, as all you have to do is hold it against the teeth while the brush does all the work. Sometimes with a manual brush, you may brush too hard and cause the gums to bleed.

Never use human toothpaste or mouthwash on your cat's teeth, because cats cannot spit and human toothpaste that contains toxic fluoride will be swallowed. There are many flavored cat toothpastes available at the pet store or veterinarian's office.

Also, it's a good idea to get your cat used to the idea of occasionally having their teeth scraped or scaled, especially the back molars which tend to build up plaque. Be very careful if you are doing this yourself, because the tools are sharp.

When your cat is a young kitten, take the time to get them used to having their mouth handled and your fingers rubbing their teeth and gums.

Next, buy some feline toothpaste at your local pet store specially flavored to appeal to cats and apply this to your cat's teeth with your finger.

Then slowly introduce the manual or electric toothbrush to your cat. When you go slowly, they will get used to the buzzing and vibrating of the electric brush, which will do a superior job of cleaning their teeth.

First, let them see the electric brush, then let them hear it buzzing, and before you put it in their mouth, let them feel the buzzing sensation on their body, while you move it slowly toward their head and muzzle.

When your cat will allow you to touch their muzzle while the brush is turned on, the next step is to lift their lip and quickly brush a couple of teeth at a time, until they get used to having them all brushed at the same time.

Always happily praise them for allowing you to brush their teeth, especially when they are first getting used to the idea.

A simple home solution for helping to keep your cat's breath fresh and their teeth white is Bicarbonate of Soda (baking soda). Simply sprinkle some into a dish and dip your finger or toothbrush first in water and then into the Bicarbonate of Soda. Then use this to clean your cat's teeth and massage their gums. Some cats seem to object less to this procedure when you use your finger.

Whether you let the electric toothbrush do the work for you or you are using your finger or a manual toothbrush, make certain that you brush in a circular motion and when using a brush, angle the bristles so that they extend underneath the gums to help prevent plaque build-up, gum disease and loose teeth.

d) Teeth Scaling: use of a tooth scraper or scaling tool once or twice a month can help to remove plaque build-up. Most accumulation will be found on the outside of the teeth and on the back molars, near or underneath the gum line.

Go slowly and carefully because these tools are sharp and only do this when your cat is calm and relaxed, a little bit at a time.

e) Healthy Teeth Tips: despite what most cat owners might put up with as normal, it is <u>not</u> normal for your cat to have smelly cat breath or feline halitosis.

Bad breath is the first sign of an unhealthy mouth, which could involve gum disease or tooth decay. There are many options available and the following tips will help keep your cat's mouth and teeth healthy:

Hydrogen Peroxide – keep your cat's teeth sparkling white and their breath fresh by using old-fashioned hydrogen peroxide as your cat "toothpaste".

Hydrogen peroxide is what is in the human whitening toothpaste. There will be such a small amount on the brush that it will not harm your cat and will kill any bacteria in your cat's mouth.

Toothpaste – many feline toothpastes are formulated with active enzymes to help keep tartar build-up at bay.

Dental Gel – it may work to help keep your cat's teeth in good health. Apparently, all you need to do is apply the gel to your cat's teeth daily and the enzymes contained in the gel will kill germs that cause tooth decay, gum disease and plaque or tartar build-up.

Dental Chews or Treats – feed a daily dental chew to help to remove tartar, while exercising the jaws and massaging the gums. Some dental chews contain natural breath freshening cinnamon, cloves or chlorophyll.

Drinking Water Additives: these have been in the marketplace for some time now and usually contain enzymes that may or may not effectively reduce plaque.

Keep in mind that these additives may alter the taste of the water, which means the cat may refuse to drink it, so keep an eye on the water dish.

Coconut Oil – helps to prevent smelly cat breath, while giving your cat's digestive, immune and metabolic functions a boost at the same time. Add ¼ teaspoon to your cat's dinner and their breath will soon be much sweeter.

Whatever you decide to do to help keep your cat's teeth healthy, you will be actively doing what is best for your cat's health by ensuring that care of their teeth is a daily routine.

6. Skin Care

Keeping your cat's coat clean and free from mats, debris and parasites by occasionally bathing with feline shampoo and conditioner, as well as providing plenty of clean water and feeding them a high-quality diet free from allergy-causing ingredients, will go a long way toward keeping their skin healthy and itch-free and their coat shiny and healthy looking.

Between bath times, there are many moist cat wipes on the market that are especially formulated with the correct pH balance to help keep your cat clean and their skin healthy.

Consider getting into the habit of choosing a wipe that is natural and has no chemical scents added, so that you can safely wipe down your cat with one of these moist towels every night before bed.

7. Pest Control

a) Fleas: every cat usually picks up a flea or two sometime in their lifetime, so you should be prepared for this inevitability by ensuring that you always have a good flea shampoo on hand.

If you notice your cat biting, scratching or chewing at his or herself, the chances that they have picked up a flea or two is quite high, so it's time for a flea bath.

b) Ticks: if your cat goes roaming freely through wooded and bushy areas with large trees, they may also pick up the occasional tick and you will have to carefully check.

Always carefully check through your cat's coat and ears after they have been romping through the woods and make sure that you also have a solution at hand that will kill a tick or the proper tool that can easily and safely twist any size of tick out of a cat's skin.

A very effective product (which is 100% safe for humans and animals) that will kill ticks on contact is a natural pest control product made by CedarCide called *"Best Yet Organic Bug Spray"*.

Pet Protector is a 100% safe tag containing no chemicals whatsoever (lasting for 4 years) that your cat or dog wears on their collar. This tag emits a charge with a specific combination of Magnetic and Scalar waves, which after being triggered by the animal's movement (blood circulation), produces an invisible energy field around the entire animal's body, so that fleas and other crawly pests won't jump on board.

Ticks can also be quickly and easily removed with a simple to use *"Tick Twister"* or a quick spray of CedarCide.

8. Brushing & Combing

An often overlooked task, that is a necessary part of maintaining the health of a cat, is daily brushing and combing.

As well, taking time to brush and comb your cat's coat will give you an opportunity to bond with your cat, while identifying any problems (such as fatty lumps or bumps and matted hair) early on (before they may become more serious).

Make sure that your grooming sessions are as pleasant as possible by choosing the right tools for your cat and their type and length of coat.

Depending on the length of your cat's coat, you will need minimal brushes and combs to keep your cat's coat in good condition, and these tools may include a slicker brush, a bristle brush, a comb and a flea comb.

9. Equipment Required

A slicker brush has short, thin, wire bristles arranged closely together and anchored to a flat (often rectangular) surface that's attached to a handle and is an ideal grooming tool for helping to remove mats and tangles from a cat that has a longer coat. Slicker brushes are often used as a finishing brush after brushing with the bristle brush to smooth the cat's coat and create a shiny finish.

A bristle brush can be used to help remove debris and dead hair from the coat and also to help distribute natural oils to keep the coat looking healthy and shiny.

A metal comb can also be used for grooming a cat. Most metal combs have a combination of widely spaced and narrow spaced teeth and are designed so that if you run into a tangle, you can switch to the wider spaced teeth while you work it out without pulling and irritating your cat.

NOTE: Some combs have rotating teeth which makes the process of removing tangles from your cat's coat much easier on them without the pain of pulling and snagging.

Mat splitters are, as the name suggests, designed to split apart matted fur on cats with longer coats so that you can then comb out the areas.

Hopefully, your daily grooming routine will mean that your cat never gets mats in their coat. However, if you are not as vigilant as might be necessary to maintain your cat's coat, mats can quickly occur underneath the belly, in the armpits and tail area or around the neck and behind the cat's ears (especially if they are wearing a collar).

Flea combs, as the name suggests, are designed for the specific purpose of removing fleas from a cat's coat. A flea comb is usually small in size for manoeuvring in tight spaces and may be made of plastic or metal with the teeth of the comb placed very close together to trap hiding fleas.

A Tick Twister is a simple device for painlessly, easily and quickly removing ticks that have imbedded themselves in your cat's skin.

Nail scissors will need to be used every couple of weeks or more, depending on how quickly your cat's nails grow, to snip off the curved end of your cat's nails.

10. Products

Shampoos: NEVER make the mistake of using human shampoo or conditioner for bathing your Scottish Fold, because cats have a different pH balance than humans.

For example, shampoo for humans has a pH balance of 5.5, whereas shampoo formulated for our feline companions has an almost neutral pH balance of 7.5.

Any shampoo with a lower pH balance will be harmful to your cat, because it will be too harshly acidic for their coat and skin, which can create skin problems.

Always purchase a shampoo for your cat that is specially formulated to be gentle and moisturizing on your cat's coat and skin, that will not strip the natural oils, and which will nourish the coat to give it a healthy shine.

As a general rule, make sure that you read the instructions provided on the shampoo bottle and avoid shampoos containing insecticides or harsh chemicals.

If your cat is suffering from an infestation of fleas, you may want to bathe them with shampoo containing pyrethrum (a botanical extract found in small, white daisies) or a shampoo containing citrus or tea tree oil, or bath and spray them with the very effective CedarCide products (which can also be used to spray down their bedding and any carpets in the home).

Conditioners: while many of us use conditioner after we shampoo our own hair, a large number of feline guardians forget to use conditioner on their own cat's coat after bathing.

Even if the bathing process is one that you wish to complete as quickly as possible, you will want to reconsider this little oversight because, just as conditioning our human hair improves its condition, the same is true for our cat's coat.

Conditioning your cat's coat will not only make it look and feel better, conditioning will also add additional benefits, including:

- Preventing the escape of natural oils and moisture
- Keeping the coat cleaner for a longer period of time
- Repairing a coat that has become damaged or dry
- Restoring a soft, silky feel
- Helping the coat dry more quickly
- Protection from the heat of the dryer and breakage of hair

Unless you are using a two-in-one shampoo plus conditioner, spend the extra two minutes to condition your cat's coat after bathing. The benefits of doing so will be appreciated by both yourself and your cat that will have overall healthy skin and a coat with a natural shine.

Styptic Powder: you will always want to avoid causing any pain when trimming your cat's toenails, because you don't want to destroy their trust in you regularly performing this necessary task.

However, accidents do happen, therefore if you accidentally cut into the vein in the toenail, know that you will cause your cat pain and that the toenail will bleed. Therefore, it is always a good idea to keep some styptic powder (often called *"Kwik Stop")* in your grooming kit.

Dip a moistened finger into the powder and apply it with pressure to the end of the bleeding nail, because this is quickest way to stop a nail from bleeding in just a few seconds.

Ear Powders: which can be purchased at any pet store, are designed to help keep your cat's ears dry while at the same time inhibiting the growth of bacteria that can lead to infections.

Ear Cleaning Solutions: your local pet store will offer a wide variety of ear cleaning creams, drops, oils, rinses or wipes specially formulated for cleaning your cat's ears. As well, there are many home remedies that will just as efficiently clean your cat's ears without the high price tag.

NOTE: because a cat's ears are a very sensitive area, always read the labels before purchasing products and avoid any solutions that list alcohol or any harsh chemical components as the main ingredient.

Home Ear Cleaning Solutions: the following are three effective home solutions that will efficiently clean your cat's ears:

Witch Hazel is a natural anti-inflammatory product that works well to cleanse and protect against infection while encouraging faster healing of minor skin traumas.

A 50:50 solution of Organic Apple Cider Vinegar and Purified Water has been used as an external folk medicine for decades. This mixture is a gentle and effective solution that kills germs while naturally healing.

A 50:50 solution of Hydrogen Peroxide and Purified Water is useful for cleansing wounds and dissolving earwax.

Whatever product you decide to use for cleaning your cat's ears, always be careful about what you put into your cat's ears and thoroughly dry them after cleaning.

Feline Toothpastes: when it comes time to brush a cat's teeth, this is where many guardians fail miserably by often using the excuse that *"my cat doesn't like it"*.

Whether they like it or otherwise is not the issue, because in order to keep your cat healthy, they <u>must</u> have healthy teeth and the only way to ensure this is to brush their teeth every day. Get into the habit of tending to the health of your cat's teeth every day and they will live a longer, much healthier life.

The many feline toothpastes on the market are usually flavored with beef or chicken in an attempt to appeal to the cat's taste buds, while others may be infused with mint or some other breath-freshening ingredient in an attempt to appeal to humans by improving the cat's breath.

Your cat is not likely going to be begging for you to brush his or her teeth no matter how tasty the paste might be. Therefore, effectiveness in the shortest period of time will be more of a deciding factor than whether or not your cat prefers the taste of the toothpaste.

Some cat toothpastes contain baking soda, which is the same mild abrasive found in many human pastes and they are designed to gently scrub the teeth. However, just how much time you will have to spend scrubbing your cat's teeth before they've had enough may be too minimal to make these pastes very effective.

Other types of feline toothpastes are formulated with enzymes that are designed to work chemically by breaking down tartar or plaque in the cat's mouth. While these pastes do not need to be washed off your cat's teeth and are safe for them to swallow, whether or not they remain on the cat's teeth long enough to do any good might be debatable.

Old-fashioned hydrogen peroxide cleans while killing germs and keeping teeth white. Just dip your cat's toothbrush in a capful of hydrogen peroxide, shake off the excess and brush their teeth. There will be such a small amount in your cat's mouth, that you don't need to worry about them swallowing it.

Organic Pest Control: CedarCide is a company that makes 100% safe, organic products to control biting bugs on your furry friends without worrying about harmful chemicals that are not good for you, your children or your feline companions.

Simply spray it on and bugs of any sort that come into contact with the solution will be dead, while your cat's coat will be shiny and fresh smelling, like the inside of a cedar chest.

11. Professional Grooming

If you decide that you are not interested in bathing or grooming your cat yourself, you will want to locate a trusted professional service to do this for you and the best way to find a groomer is to ask others who they use and whether they are happy with the results.

An average price for professionally bathing and brushing a cat may be between $15 and $25 (£11 and £18) and could be considerably more depending upon the size of the cat, the length of their coat, the condition of their coat, how calmly they accept the procedure and whether the salon is also trimming nails or brushing teeth.

Chapter 15: Socializing Your Cat

Most cats, when properly and continually socialized, will be tolerant of other cats, people and other household pets, such as the family dog, which they will usually learn to play with if introduced as kittens or carefully and slowly integrated as an adult.

Without socialization and exposure to different people, animals, places and unfamiliar sights and sounds when they are kittens, your cat may become fearful, timid, nervous, skittish or aggressive around unfamiliar sights and sounds.

Much of how any cat behaves will depend entirely upon you, how much time you took to socialize them as a kitten and how much they are continually being socialized throughout their life. A well-socialized cat will be much more likely to be loving, trusting, friendly and well balanced.

Never make the mistake of thinking that you only need to socialize a young kitten and then they will be fine for the rest of their life. Any cat that does not continue to be regularly socialized may become shy or suspicious of unfamiliar or unusual people or circumstances, which could lead to nervous or fearful behavior, which can then lead a cat to act out aggressively.

1. With Other Cats and Pets

Generally speaking, the majority of an adult cat's habits and behavioral traits will be formed between the ages of birth and six months of age.

This is why it will be very important to introduce your kitten to a wide variety of sights, sounds, smells and situations during the most formative period in their young life, which is usually the first 16 weeks.

Your kitten will learn how to behave in all these various circumstances by following your lead, feeling your energy and watching your body language and how you react in every situation.

For instance, never accidentally reward your kitten or cat for displaying nervousness, fear, scratching or growling at another cat, animal or person by picking them up.

Picking up a kitten or cat at a time when they are displaying unbalanced energy actually turns out to be a reward for them and you will be teaching them to continue with this type of behavior.

The correct action to take in such a situation is to gently correct your kitten with a firm yet calm energy by distracting them with a "No" or a snap of your fingers to get their attention back on you, so that they learn to let you deal with the situation on their behalf.

If you allow a fearful, nervous or shy kitten deal with situations that unnerve them without your direction, they may learn to react with fear or aggression to unfamiliar circumstances and you will have created a problem that could escalate into something more serious as they grow older.

The same is true of situations where a young kitten may feel the need to protect itself from a larger or older cat or a dog that may come charging in for a sniff. It is the guardian's responsibility to protect the kitten, so that they do not feel that they must react with fear or aggression in order to protect themselves.

Once your kitten has received all their vaccinations, they can interact with other cats or kittens. If you plan to travel with your cat, you will want to train them to a kennel and take them for a drive and/or walk them outside on a leash and harness, so they learn about the great outdoors and some of the sights and sounds that are associated with it.

Keep a close watch on your Scottish Fold kitten to make sure they are not being overwhelmed by other cats, children or people, or getting overly excited and stressed or nervous, because it is your job to protect your kitten.

If your kitten shows any signs of aggression or domination toward another kitten, cat or person, you must immediately step in and calmly discipline them. Otherwise, by doing nothing you will be agreeing with their behavior and will be allowing them to learn to be aggressive when they find themselves in unfamiliar situations.

No matter the age or size of your kitten, allowing them to display aggression or domination over another cat or growl and scratch a person or other animal is never a laughing matter and if you want to raise a well-balanced cat, this type of behavior must be immediately curtailed.

2. With Other People

If you are planning to travel with your cat, you will want to take your kitten everywhere with you and introduce them to many different people and circumstances, so they will learn what is normal and can relax. This will be easy to do, because most people will automatically be drawn to you when they see you have a kitten.

Most humans will want to interact with your kitten and if they ask to hold him or her, this is an ideal opportunity to socialize your kitten around many different ages, sexes and ethnicities and show them that humans are friendly.

Do not let others (especially young children) play roughly with your kitten or squeal at them in a high-pitched voice, because this can be very frightening for a young kitten. You do not want to teach your kitten that humans are a source of loud, unpredictable energy that they should fear.

Be especially careful when introducing your kitten to young children who may accidentally hurt your kitten, because you don't want them to grow into a cat that is fearful of children as this could lead to aggression issues later on in life.

Explain to children that your kitten is very young and that they must be calm and gentle when playing or interacting in any way.

3. Within Different Environments

It can be a big mistake not to take the time to introduce your Scottish Fold kitten to a wide variety of different environments, because when they are not comfortable with different sights and sounds this could cause them possible trauma later in their adult life, especially if you plan to travel with your cat.

Be creative, buy a carrier and take your kitten everywhere you can imagine when they are young so that no matter where they travel, whether strolling along a noisy city sidewalk or beside a peaceful shoreline, they will be equally comfortable.

Do not make the mistake of only taking your kitten into areas where you live and will always travel, because they need to also be comfortable visiting areas you might not often visit, such as an airport or a shopping area across town.

Your kitten needs to see all sorts of sights, sounds and situations, so that they will not become fearful should they need to travel with you to any of these areas.

Your kitten will take their cues from you, which means that when you are calm and in control of every situation and they have a comfortable carrier to travel in, they will learn to be calm and accepting of many different circumstances.

For instance, take them to the airport where they can watch people and hear planes landing and taking off or take them to a local park where there is a soccer game in progress, or for a stroll beside a schoolyard at recess time when noisy children are out playing, or take them to the local zoo or farm and let them get a close up look at horses, pigs and ducks.

Again, never think that socialization is something that only takes place when your cat is a young kitten, as proper socialization is on-going for your cat's entire life.

When you do not take the time to socialize your cat, they may spend their life hiding under the bed.

4. Loud Noises

Many cats can show extreme fear of loud noises, such as fireworks or thunderstorms.

When you take the time to desensitize your cat to these types of noises when they are very young, it will be much easier on them during stormy weather or holidays such as Halloween or New Year's when fireworks are often a part of the festivities.

You can purchase CD's that are a collection of unusual sounds, such as vacuums or hoovers, airplanes, sirens, smoke alarms, fireworks, people clapping hands, screaming children, and more (or you can easily make your own), that you can play while working in your kitchen or relaxing in your living room or lounge.

First, play these sounds softly and then slowly increase the volume until the cat no longer seems affected by these noises. When you play these sounds and pretend that everything is normal, the next time your kitten or cat hears these types of sounds elsewhere, they will not become as upset or agitated because they have learned to ignore them.

Bubble wrap is also another simple way to desensitize a cat that is fearful of popping sounds. Show them the bubble wrap, pop a few of the cells and if they do not run away, give them a treat. You can start with the bubble wrap that has small, quieter cells and then graduate them to the larger celled (louder) bubble wrap.

Also, make sure that you get your young kitten used to the sounds of thunder and fireworks at an early age. These types of shrieking, crashing, banging and popping sounds of fireworks or thunder (as well as the high-pitched beeping of household smoke and fire alarms) can be so traumatic and unsettling for many cats, that sometimes, no matter how much you try to calm your cat or pretend that everything is fine, there is little you can do.

Some cats literally lose their minds when they hear the loud popping or screeching noises of fireworks and alarms and start trembling, running or trying to hide and you cannot communicate with them at all.

Make sure that your cat cannot harm itself trying to escape from these types of noises, and if possible, hold them until they begin to relax or place them in one room where they can be safe.

If your cat has not been desensitized to these types of noises and loses its mind when it hears them, simply avoid taking them anywhere near fireworks. At times when they might hear these noises going off outside, play your inside music or TV louder than you might normally to help disguise the exterior noise of fireworks or thunder.

Do not underestimate the importance of taking the time to continually (not just when they are kittens) socialize and desensitize your kitten to all manner of sights, sounds, individuals and locations. To do so will be teaching them to be a calm and well-balanced member of your family that will not live in fear every time they hear a loud noise.

Chapter 16: Training Your Scottish Fold Cat

1. Trainability

Even though most people think that cats cannot be trained, it's actually quite easy to train a cat, for instance, to come on command and the easiest way to do this is with a simple clicker and treat formula.

Some cats can learn to do amazing tricks and some of them will even learn how to do tricks without any training from their humans. For example, I once had a cat that would retrieve paper airplanes, which was very entertaining for both cat and human.

Keep in mind that a cat is NOT a dog and a cat will <u>not</u> learn from "disciplining" or "punishing" them for the behavior you want to dissuade. The Scottish Fold is a highly intelligent cat that is easy to train and quick to learn.

Never use harsh treatment toward your cat because doing so can easily cause stress and create a nervous or fearful cat, which can then lead to health issues and more behavioral issues.

Positive reinforcement and endless patience is essential when training a cat.

While practice makes perfect, always keep in mind that each cat (and human) is different, which means that realistically the time it takes to train a cat can vary greatly from them getting it after just a few tries to practicing for several weeks before the light bulb goes off.

Training your kitten or cat to learn a new skill will entirely depend on both your cat's temperament, personality and willingness to learn and your calm patience and persistence.

a) Clicker Training

When you want to train your cat to come to you, all you have to do is teach them to associate something they like (i.e., a really enticing treat) with the sound of the clicker. Be sure to use treats your cat goes crazy for whenever you are training.

Before you begin, you will have to *"charge"* the clicker, meaning teaching your cat that when they hear the sound of the clicker, they get a tasty treat. So, before you begin teaching a specific trick, simply click the clicker and immediately give your cat a treat.

After doing this a few times, your cat will quickly learn that when they hear the sound of the clicker, they are going to get a tasty reward.

Start training from short distances – click the clicker and when your cat comes, reward him or her with the treat. Then use the same formula while gradually extending the distance.

Begin with 2-3 short training sessions and practice each day for about five minutes each session. Over time, you will be able to teach your cat to come running from longer and longer distances.

Once they associate the click sound with receiving a treat, all you have to do is click the clicker to get your cat's attention and when they come to you, give them the treat (good kitty!). Also, the clicker can be used in a variety of training scenarios.

b) Leash Training

Training your kitten or cat to walk on a leash means that you can both enjoy time together outdoors without worrying that your cat might run off in the wrong direction and get themselves into trouble. This breed enjoys learning tricks and may also be easy to train to walk on a leash and harness.

Before you begin, you will need to purchase a harness and leash and then slowly introduce it to your kitten or cat by first just letting them see and sniff it (leave it in their bed where they get used to seeing it), and then drape it over them without actually putting it on, and give a treat.

The first time you put the harness on, they will usually try to get it off, so have a treat and a toy handy to distract them with and only put the harness on them for short periods of time until they get used to how it feels on their body.

Once they stop trying to squirm their way out of the harness, you can attach the leash and let them drag it around the house (under your supervision) for a couple of minutes. This way, they will get used to the feeling of the leash having some control over where they can wander.

After your kitten or cat is comfortable with wearing their harness and dragging the leash about the house, you can start holding the leash and following them, only applying slight restraint and soon they will associate the pull of the leash with you being in control.

The next step in your cat's leash training will be to slowly transition them into the great outdoors. Perhaps just a walk around your back yard will be sufficient to begin with, after which you might venture down your driveway together.

Remember that being in the great outdoors is a very new and big adventure for a cat that has never been outside before, so don't overwhelm them with being out there for too long and always be vigilant and aware of other animals (such as the neighbor's dog) that may frighten them.

Choose a quiet time of the day and an area where there is not a lot of traffic, so that your cat can take his or her time sniffing and exploring a new area without being shocked by loud vehicle traffic or barking dogs.

What you can teach your cat depends entirely upon you and the time and patience you have to devote to their education and not on what some expert might tell you with respect to how smart this particular breed may or may not be.

For instance, if you are patient and your cat is enjoying learning new tricks, there are many things you can learn together, such as "Sit", "High Five", "Shake", "Jump Through a Hoop", "Fetch", negotiate an obstacle course, or even to close cabinet doors for you.

No matter what you decide to teach your cat, always train with patience and kindness and NEVER yell, hit or punish a cat during training or at any time for that matter.

Stay calm when training and keep your sessions short until your cat becomes accustomed to new routines.

c) Toilet Training

Some people believe that teaching a cat to use a human toilet is contrary to what a cat is *"wired"* to use as a bathroom, which is their natural propensity for digging a hole and covering it over once finished. While this is certainly true, I can tell you from personal experience that cats can be trained to use the toilet.

While it may take some patience to get the results you desire, there are definitely plenty of benefits to enjoy once you succeed, including the obvious ones being that you no longer have to purchase cat litter or clean the box, which means a cleaner home without the tell-tale odors of cat urine and feces.

As every cat will naturally want to do their business in a litter box, when training them to use the human toilet, the first step will be to simply place their box beside the toilet that you want to transition them to.

Next, gradually raise their litter box to the top of the toilet seat and if they are very young, you may need to build a ramp or step stool so they can get to their raised box.

IMPORTANT: make sure that the raised litter box is stable, because if the whole arrangement falls over and goes crashing to the floor, not only will you have a big mess to clean up but you will also have a frightened cat, who may now be afraid to use the elevated box (which may set them back in their training).

Once you have the cat used to using a litter box that is at the same height as the toilet, you will simply place the cat's litter box on top of the closed toilet seat. After they are used to this, the next step will be to change from their traditional litter box to a special training box that has several stages and is actually is designed to fit within the toilet seat *("CitiKitty"* or *"Litter Kwitter").*

At this stage of your cat's toilet training, you will want to use flushable litter and then slowly use less and less litter, which will get your kitten or cat used to doing their business without using any litter. Once this is accomplished, you can remove the training box completely.

With patience, you can also teach your cat to flush the toilet after they are done. How long will all this training take, you might ask? While the answer, of course, will vary because each cat (and human) is different, any cat can learn to use the human toilet, whether you started your cat with this training as a kitten or he or she is already an adult cat.

While an average timeframe for totally toilet training your cat might be 2 to 3 weeks (no matter what you are teaching), all training sessions should be happy and fun-filled with plenty of treat rewards and positive reinforcement. which will ensure that your cat is an attentive student who looks forward to learning new commands, tricks and routines.

2. Kitten Training Basics

Most humans believe that they need to take their young cat to kitten classes and, generally speaking, this is a good idea for any young cat (after they have had all their vaccinations), because it will help to get them socialized.

Beyond kitten classes for socialization reasons, hiring a professional cat whisperer for personalized private sessions to train the humans may be far more valuable than training situations where there are multiple cats and humans together in one class, as this can be very distracting for everyone concerned.

a) Crate Training

I cannot stress strongly enough how important and valuable it will be to train your kitten or cat to calmly accept crate training.

This is not only a good idea because you may want to travel with your cat in the future, but it is also a good idea if the only time you travel with your cat is when they go to the vet's office for their yearly check-up.

A cat that has not been taught to calmly accept their crate as a safe haven, will be extremely stressed when you stuff them in there and put them in your vehicle because all of this is so unfamiliar to them that their stress level will be off the scale.

Some cats become so stressed and afraid when placed in a crate and transported to (for instance) the vet's office, that they will scream, wail and let loose their bowels.

b) Training Sound

Every cat needs to associate a human sound with the idea that they must cease and desist from doing something you don't want them to do and a sound that is very effective for most cats and kittens is a simple *"UH"* sound said sharply and with emphasis, or a loud *"PSSSST"*.

Most kittens and cats respond immediately to sharp sounds and if caught in the middle of doing something they are not supposed to be doing, they will quickly stop and give you their attention or back away from what they were doing.

Of course, you can choose any sound that you find effective so long as you and all family members consistently use this for getting your cat's attention and interrupting unwanted behavior.

c) House Rules

When you first bring a new kitten or cat into your home, it will be important to quickly establish basic house rules so that they learn what is acceptable and what is not.

For instance, when your kitten correctly learns that certain areas are off limits to them (such as the kitchen stove or countertop or the dining room table where the humans eat), you will avoid possible injury and keep your food preparation areas sanitary.

All that's necessary for effectively teaching your kitten their basic first house rules is a calm, consistent approach, combined with your endless patience.

Many kittens are ready to begin training at about 10 to 12 weeks of age, however, be careful not to overdo it when they are less than four to six months of age, as their attention span will be short.

Make your training sessions no more than 5 or 10 minutes, positive and pleasant, with lots of praise and/or treats so that your kitten will be looking forward to their next session.

If you have the time and the patience, there are many fun routines, tricks and commands you can teach a willing cat.

d) The Come Command

While most kittens will be capable of learning commands and tricks at a young age, the first and most important command you need to teach your kitten is to come to you when called (discussed earlier in this Chapter, under Clicker Training).

Begin the "Come" command inside your home. Go into a large room, such as your living room area. Place your kitten in front of you and have special treats at the ready.

Say the command "Come" in a happy voice, click the clicker and give the treat. Slowly increase the distance between you and your kitten while repeating the exercise and when they come to you praise them and immediately give a treat they really enjoy.

Once your kitten can accomplish a "Come" command almost every time inside your home, you can then graduate them to your back yard or a quiet outside area where you will repeat the process.

e) The Sit Command

The "Sit" command is an easy command to teach a cat or kitten and you will need to find a quiet time to teach this command when your kitten is not overly tired or distracted by other commotion going on around them.

Get your kitten's attention with the clicker and when they come to you, say the word "Sit" while holding a favorite treat above their head. They will usually sit to look up and see what they want and when they do, immediately give them the treat.

Can you teach a cat hand signals? Of course, you can and the good news is that if you are interested in advancing your cat's training to hand signals, it's quite easy to do.

For instance, when you say the word "Sit", at the same time show your cat the hand signal for this command. While you can use any hand signal, the universal hand signal for "Sit" is:

Right arm (palm open facing upward) parallel to the floor and then raising your arm, while bent at the elbow toward your right shoulder.

Once your cat is sitting reliably for you, you can remove the clicker sound and the verbal "Sit" and replace it with the hand signal. How cool is that?

If you also want to teach the "Come" command with hand signals, the universal silent signal for "Come" is arms outstretched in a wide, open stance, like you are hugging a large tree.

While you can begin teaching hand signals at any stage of a cat's life, you might want to get a kitten used to this type of training early on, because this will also help them to be more attentive and communicate in a way that is more natural for a cat — by watching you and feeling your energy, rather than always having to hear a clicker or you speaking a command.

When you ask your kitten to "Sit" before you interact in any way with them (such as before you feed them), you are helping to quiet their mind, while teaching them to look to you for direction.

Make your training sessions short (5 minutes) until your kitten gets older and their attention span increases, at which time you may be able to train for longer periods of time, so long as your cat is still interested.

f) Leash Training Your Kitten

Leash training has been discussed earlier in this Chapter. While a cat of any age can be trained to accept a harness and leash, if you are bringing a new kitten into your home, teaching them to accept a harness and leash will be much easier for everyone if you begin this process when they are still a kitten.

3. Adult Training

When your cat is a full-grown adult (approximately one year of age), you will definitely want to begin more complicated or advanced training sessions.

For instance, you may wish to teach your adult cat more advanced tricks, such as how to high five, jump up or the opposite-sided paw shakes or rollovers (which are more difficult than you might expect), or even to run an Agility course.

All of these tricks and more are fun to teach and will exercise both your cat's mind and body by taking advantage of their natural curiosity and athletic ability. The only restriction with respect to how far you can go with training your adult cat, will be your imagination and their personal ability or desire to perform.

4. Behavioral Issues

It can be difficult (if not impossible) to generalize or speculate with respect to alleviating possible behavioral issues or problems you may encounter with your cat because, in most cases, a cat suffering from behavioral issues requires the assistance of a cat whisperer or cat psychologist.

When reading anything about how to prevent or cure behavioral issues, please be aware that behavioral problems most often cannot be properly assessed or cured by reading a book.

The reason for this is because there are just too many variables and unique situations, individual cats, individual humans, unique circumstances, and endless reasons why they may have developed any particular behavioral issue.

Therefore, without knowing the cat's particulars and all the history of what has transpired between a particular cat and their guardian that came before or how the problem might have manifested itself, attempting to write about how to cure a particular issue will be no more than a best guess.

This is why someone whose cat is suffering from a specific behavioral issue will usually need the assistance of a competent, professional who can ask many questions, properly assess the situation and then design a unique plan for alleviating the problem.

Chapter 17: The Unruly Adolescent

What happened to my sweet, little kitten?

Sometime between the age of 6 months to 1 ½ years, while it may seem like *"all of a sudden"*, your adorable kitten has grown into a cat that has become difficult to live with. Your kitten has been slowly and silently transitioning into what humans call the *"terrible teens"*, which in the cat world is simply feline adolescence.

When our kittens begin to mature into adult cats (like a teenager), they will have excess energy, a desire to test their boundaries with other animals and you and to make their place in the world known to all around them. What they do during this stage of their life may not exactly fit with how you imagined your life might be with your cat.

Some of the behaviors you might experience with your adolescent cat could include them using their claws to modify the arms of your favorite couch or chair which leaves scent markings, and picking fights with the neighborhood cats.

If you have an indoor cat, they may display their displeasure at being caged inside your home by jumping higher than you thought possible to find better vantage points, which could include the top of the fridge or that expensive china cabinet where you keep all the fragile crystal glassware.

The adolescent phase in a young cat's life is also the time when they attain sexual maturity, which means that a female cat will scream and howl her availability to prospective suitors, while the tomcat male equivalent will swagger their way through the neighborhood fighting with other males, while searching for available females to mate with.

In order to more quietly pass through this stage of your cat's life and eliminate a stage that can start up a habit of marking and spraying furniture, it is often recommended that kittens are spayed or neutered at the age of 3 or 4 months.

If your kitten happens to be especially unruly or belligerent during their adolescent phase, you will need to simply provide them with more outlets for safely exercising and releasing their energy while limiting their opportunities for making mistakes.

For instance, it does absolutely no good to yell at your cat for engaging in behavior you are not happy with, and in fact, yelling or getting angry will only desensitize your young cat from listening to any of your commands. Although you may eventually get the results you want if you yell loud enough, your kitten will then be reacting out of fear, rather than respect, and this will be damaging to your relationship.

Rather, be aware of what is possible during this phase of your kitten's life, so that you can both survive the process relatively unscathed by channelling your young cat's energy through daily play time, trick training or interesting, interactive puzzle toys that will keep the brain engaged and the body occupied.

If a young cat is particularly aggressive and is "attacking" your legs, hands or other body parts in overly fierce play, you can sharply say, "*No*", hiss sharply at him or her and walk away.

Also, (if you don't already have one) a cat tower or combination tower and scratching post will help by giving your cat the opportunity to scratch and climb and when you have the patience to teach tricks, this is a good way to redirect that excess of energy into learning something new.

The best thing you can do to help your young cat transition through their adolescent phase of life is to be educated, stay calm, understand what to expect and keep your sense of humor, because just as "suddenly" as your sweet kitten turned into an uncontrollable Tasmanian devil, they will turn back into that well-behaved cat that you were looking forward to sharing your life with.

Displaying calm, yet assertive energy is the ONLY energy that works well to help your adolescent kitten understand what is required of them, and you getting angry with them will only make matters worse.

An extremely rambunctious adolescent cat may need to have their free run of the house curtailed, especially if they have decided to turn all your curtains into rags, so that they are confined to areas where you can easily supervise them.

Make sure they are within eyesight at all times, so that if they do find an opportunity to make a mistake, you can quickly show them what is permitted and what is not.

Adolescence may also be a time when you might have to insist that your young companion sleeps in their crate with the door closed whenever you cannot supervise, as well as at bedtime so they continue to understand that you have firm rules.

As well, keeping on top of house training is also a good idea during the adolescent period of your kitten's life, because some adolescent kittens may become stubborn and forget that they are already litter box or toilet trained and may instead decide to do their business in your favorite shoes.

Don't worry and stay calm, because your previous training will return.

1. Giving Up is Not an Option

Too often we humans get frustrated and give up on our cats when they change from being the cute, cuddly and mostly sweet, little kitten they once were and become all kinds of trouble you never bargained for as they grow into their adolescent stage.

Many times, it will be during the confusing adolescent stage of a cat's life that they find themselves abandoned and left behind bars as their humans, who promised to love and protect them, leave their once loved fur friend at the local cat pound, SPCA or rescue facility.

First of all, not all cats go through such an intense adolescent period. Secondly, even if they do (please read this section carefully), you can live through kitten adolescence and come out the other side relatively unscathed and a much more knowledgeable and patient guardian.

Also, remember to be proud of your socializing and training accomplishments thus far in your cat's life and all that you and your kitten have accomplished together over the last several months.

Even though your adolescent kitten may be starting to act like a Tasmanian devil and you might be having second thoughts, now is not the time to give up on them and yourself just because it may seem like someone switched your cat when you weren't looking.

Now is the time to remain calmly consistent and persistent and to know that you will eventually be able to enjoy the happy rewards that all those months of diligent kitten training have brought to your relationship.

Yes, it can be quite a shock when what used to be your well-behaved little darling (who used to sit and quietly purr in your lap) suddenly takes it into their head to pick fights and scratch everyone or knock over your precious vase collection that you thought was safely out of harm's way.

Even more disconcerting might be when your previously toilet trained kitten (who even knows how to flush the toilet and always comes when you call), suddenly appears to have gone deaf and has started to pee in your shoes, shred the couch and spray the curtains.

And then, what happened to that quiet little kitten that never appeared to have a mean bone in their body that now spends most of their time laying at wait on top of the fridge waiting to pounce on unsuspecting passers-by?

Welcome to the world of feline adolescence where it appears that your kitten has turned into some sort of monster and all your previous hard work was for nothing.

This is the time when your patience may be seriously tested. Of course, this dramatic switch from being the world's best kitten into the monster you can no longer control is not true for all kittens, as every kitten is unique.

However, being prepared for the worst will help you ride any impending tidal wave that might be on the horizon and get you both safely out the other side where you can enjoy an even closer relationship than you previously had.

Be aware that the adolescent phase may be very subtle for your kitten or on the other hand, it may be so dramatic that you're starting to feel guilty every time you drive past the local SPCA or cat pound, because thoughts of rehoming are running through your head.

If you are at the stage with your kitten that you are having great difficulties and wondering if you made the right decision to share your home with a cat, rest assured that kitten adolescence is a normal phase of their development, which can be managed and which will definitely pass.

As well, if you are finding yourself totally overwhelmed, there are many professionals who can provide valuable assistance to help you through this stage of your kitten's development.

For most kittens, adolescence will begin between the ages of five or six months and you should be considering making an appointment at your veterinarian's office to have your kitten spayed or neutered <u>before</u> this happens.

Although neutering or spaying will not completely prevent undesirable adolescent behavior, it can certainly reduce the intensity of it, as during this period there are strong hormonal changes occurring that will affect your kitten's behavior.

While it's usually hormones that are the major cause of behavioral changes in your adolescent kitten, there are also physical changes occurring at the same time that you may not be aware of.

For instance, your kitten will be going through physical growth spurts which might be causing them some pain, as well as changes related to growth in their brain while your kitten's cerebral cortex becomes more involved in thinking for itself.

Usually, during this time of brain growth, a kitten will be trying to make choices for his or herself and they may or may not yet be capable of making the <u>right</u> choices, which is why their behavior can appear to be quite erratic.

During the early adolescent period of brain development in your kitten, the signals sometimes get mixed up and rerouted, which can result in the perplexing responses you might notice, when for instance, you ask you kitten to come to you and they stare dumbly at you even though they learned this command months ago.

Also, you need to be especially careful during the often demanding adolescent phase in a young cat's life that you are not inadvertently teaching your cat bad behavior.

For example, if your cat is wailing and crying at you to get up earlier than you would prefer because they want to play, get outside, be fed or cuddle and you capitulate, you will actually be rewarding him or her for bad behavior and teaching your cat to be your boss.

Once you get into this type of routine, your cat will be certain to repeat this irritating behavior until they get what they want, so be strong and ignore your cat when they are being demanding because if you don't play, the unwanted behavior will soon stop.

Be aware that once your kitten has become a young cat, they will have developed physically as well as mentally, which means that areas of your home that were previously safe from the destructive forces of a playful kitten can now be easily accessible by a young cat who has endless energy, clueless curiosity and can jump much higher.

2. Re-think Cat Proofing

Plenty of *"accidents"* can happen when your cat becomes a delinquent adolescent who is now a combination of clumsiness and physical maturity, that can climb and jump from much greater heights, figure out how to open cupboards and doors and quickly run away when they hear footsteps approaching.

Whereas a younger, and much smaller kitten would be hard pressed to get themselves into serious troubles, a matured adolescent cat is at a considerably higher risk of injuring himself or herself, because they have excess energy, an insatiable curiosity, and the size, strength and agility of an older cat.

For instance, your older cat can now easily jump up onto countertops and hot stovetop surfaces or they can easily become locked behind doors or stuck in small holes and spaces they were innocently exploring.

Further, once a cat realizes that they can jump much higher than they could as a young kitten, there will be few places they won't want to explore or heights they won't try to conquer.

Many cats will enjoy playing games with fragile, inanimate objects that you may treasure by pushing these objects from their previously safe perch and watching them smash on the floor below. Such fun!

Also, if you thought that the beautifully decorated Christmas tree that took you and the family many hours to decorate will still be standing when you get home from work, you might want to re-think that one, especially if you have more than one indoor cat that loves to climb.

I once had two cats that together would ensure that the Christmas tree was dutifully killed and undecorated every single day while I was at work and the only way I eventually stopped this behavior was to nail the tree stand to the floor. You could hardly blame them – I mean what a delight for a cat, all those Christmas balls to bat about and all that shiny, enticing bric-a-brac.

Cat adolescence is the time that you need to seriously re-think cat proofing your entire home and this means putting away all of those precious breakables and securing them behind locked doors for their safety and for the safety of your cat who may be in danger of cutting their feet on objects they have just smashed on the floor.

Walk about your house and ask yourself, "*If I were an energetic, adolescent cat looking to get myself into mischief, what looks like an enticing possibility?*". Then when you eliminate anything that could cause trouble, you and your cat might still be friends when the adolescent crazies work their way out the other side.

3. Re-visit Kitten Training Basics

Another great thing to do once your kitten is displaying adolescent behavior is to re-visit kitten training basics (see Chapter 16), because keeping your cat occupied and their mind engaged will help greatly with the transition.

Make your training sessions no more than 5 or 10 minutes, positive and pleasant with lots of praise and/or treats, so that your kitten will be looking forward to their next session.

Also, introduce the hand signals that go along with the verbal commands, so that once they learn both, you can remove the verbal commands in favor of just hand signals.

Return to the Kitten Training Basics and go over the "Come" and "Sit" commands and everyday use these commands and any other tricks you have learned together in every opportunity, to help your young cat progress through their unpredictable adolescent period.

4. Simple Tricks

Teaching simple tricks can help a cat transition through their adolescent stage much more easily, because this will keep their mind occupied and their body exercised.

When teaching your adolescent cat tricks, in order to give them extra incentive, find a treat that they really like and give the treat as a reward and to help solidify a good performance.

Most cats will be extra attentive during training sessions, when they know that they will be rewarded with their favorite treats.

If your cat is less than six months old when you begin teaching them tricks, keep your training sessions short (no more than 5 or 10 minutes) and fun, and as they become adults, you can extend your sessions as they will be able to maintain their focus for longer periods of time.

a) Shake a Paw: yes, cats can learn how to shake a paw and this is one of the easiest tricks to teach your cat.

Most cats are naturally either right or left pawed. If you know which paw your cat favors, ask them to shake this paw. Find a quiet place to practice without noisy distractions or other pets and stand or sit in front of your cat. Place them in the sitting position and have a treat in your left hand.

Say the command *"Shake"* while putting your right hand behind their left or right paw and pulling the paw gently toward yourself until you are holding their paw in your hand. Immediately praise them and give them the treat.

Most cats will learn the "Shake" trick quite quickly and very soon once you put out your hand, your cat will immediately lift their paw and put it into your hand, without your assistance or any verbal cue.

Practice every day until they are 100% reliable with this trick and then it will be time to add another trick to their repertoire.

b) Roll Over: you will find that just as your cat is naturally either right or left pawed, they will also naturally want to roll either to the right or the left side. Take advantage of this by asking your cat to roll to the side they naturally prefer.

Sit with your cat on the floor and put them in a lie-down position. Hold a treat in your hand and place it close to their nose without allowing them to grab it. While they are in the lying position, move the treat to the right or left side of their head, so that they have to roll over to get to it.

You will very quickly see which side they want to naturally roll to and once you see this, move the treat to this side. When they roll over to this side, immediately give them the treat and praise them.

You can say the verbal cue *"Over"* while you demonstrate the hand signal motion (moving your right hand in a circular motion) or move the treat from one side of their head to the other with a half-circle motion.

c) Sit Pretty: while this trick is a little more complicated, most cats will pick up on this trick very quickly. Remember that every cat is different, so always exercise patience.

Find a quiet space with few distractions and sit or stand in front of your cat and ask them to "Sit".

Have a treat nearby (on a countertop or table) and when they sit, use both of your hands to lift up their front paws into the sitting pretty position, while saying the command *"Sit Pretty"*. Help them balance in this position, while you praise them and give them the treat.

Once your Scottish Fold can do the balancing part of the trick quite easily without your help, sit or stand in front of your cat while asking them to *"Sit Pretty"* and hold the treat above their head at the level of their nose. That would be when they sit pretty.

If they attempt to stand on their back legs to get the treat, you may be holding the treat too high, which will encourage them to stand on their back legs to reach it. Go back to the first step and put them back into the *"Sit"* position and again lift their paws while their backside remains on the floor.

Sit Pretty hand signal: hold your straight arm, fully extended, over your cat's head with a closed fist.

Make this a fun and entertaining time for both of you and practice a few times every day until they can *"Sit Pretty"* on hand signal command every time you ask.

A young kitten should be able to easily learn these basic tricks before they are six months old and when you are patient and make your training sessions short and fun for your cat, they will be eager to learn more.

Chapter 18: Foods & Plants Toxic to Cats

1. Poisonous Foods

While some cats are smart enough not to want to eat foods that can harm or kill them, there are those feline companions that will eat absolutely anything they can get their teeth on, whether or not it's food.

If your cat is highly food motivated, in order to keep them safe and healthy, it will be very important to keep cupboards containing any food or poisonous products tightly closed and out of their reach.

This will also include any area where you might store garbage because if they can smell it, they will soon figure out how to get to it.

As conscientious guardians for our furry friends, it will always be our responsibility to make certain that when we share our homes with a cat, we never leave foods (or other products) that could be toxic or lethal to them easily within their reach.

While there are many foods that can be toxic to a cat, the following alphabetical list contains some of the more common foods that can seriously harm or even kill our cats:

- Alcoholic Beverages
- Bones (from fish, poultry, etc.)
- Caffeine (from coffee, tea or chocolate)
- Canned Tuna
- Chocolate
- Citrus Oil
- Dairy Products (some cats cannot break down the lactose)
- Dog Food
- Fat Trimmings
- Grapes (& raisins)
- Garlic (in all forms)
- Iron Supplements
- Liver
- Macadamia Nuts
- Marijuana
- Mushrooms
- Onions (in all forms)
- Persimmons
- Potato
- Raw Eggs
- Raw Fish
- Rhubarb
- Salt
- Sugar
- Tobacco
- Tomato Leaves and Stems
- Yeast Dough

NOTE: Many cats are attracted to string-like objects and during play will often swallow dental floss, string, thread, tinsel and rubber bands, which can require an emergency trip to the vet's office.

If you have one of those cats who will happily eat anything that looks or smells even slightly like food (or even if not food, but is enticing for a kitten or cat to eat), be certain to keep these foods or products far away from your beloved Scottish Fold and you'll help them to live a long and healthy life.

2. Electrical Cords

Many cats also like the feel of the texture of electrical cords on their teeth and in order to prevent this unfortunate accident from occurring, you will want to encase these cords inside PVC tubing or rub them with a scent that cats will avoid, such as citrus, in order to avoid possible electrocution.

3. Flowering Plants

There is a very large number of plants that are poisonous to our cats – in fact far too many to list here. Therefore, in order to keep up to date with plants that can be harmful to your cat, you may want to check the vast listing posted at the Cat Fanciers Association website.

Many common house plants are actually poisonous to our feline companions and although many cats simply will ignore house plants, some will attempt to eat anything, especially kittens who want to taste everything in their new world.

Therefore, it is especially important to be aware of household plants that could be toxic when you are sharing your home with a new kitten.

Following is a short list of the more common household plants and cut flowers (in alphabetical order), that are potentially toxic to cats. Please note that many varieties of lilies are especially harmful and can actually cause death, which means you will want to seek immediate veterinary assistance if you believe your cat has come in contact with them:

- Amaryllis
- Asian Lily
- Autumn Crocus
- Bird of Paradise
- Climbing Lily
- Cyclamen
- Daffodil
- Day Lily
- Easter Lily
- Elephant Ear
- Gladiola
- Hydrangea
- Iris

- Kalanchoe
- Lily of the Valley
- Narcissus
- Poinsettia
- Rubrum Lily
- Stargazer Lily
- Tiger Lily
- Tulip
- Wood Lily

4. Ferns

Cats love to play with (and taste) soft, feathery ferns and you will want to be careful not to permit this behavior, because many can be toxic to a cat, including:

Asparagus Fern – Emerald Fern – Lace Fern – Plumosa Fern.

5. Indoor Plants

There are many common indoor plants that may be toxic to your cat, such as:

- Aglaonema
- Arrowhead Vine
- Dracaena Deremensis
- Dracaena Fragrans
- Dracaena Marginata

6. Perennials

Many flowering perennials plants are toxic to cats and the following alphabetical list outlines some of the more common ones:

- Aloe Vera
- Anthurium
- Arum Lily
- Calla Lily
- Hellebore
- Morning Glory
- Mother-in-Law's Tongue
- Nightshade Pussy's Ears

7. Poison Proof Your Home

You can learn about many potentially toxic and poisonous sources both inside and outside your home by visiting the ASPCA Animal Poison Control Center website.

Always keep your veterinarian's emergency number in a place where you can quickly access it, as well as the Emergency Poison Control telephone number, in case you suspect that your cat may have been poisoned.

Knowing what to do if you suspect your cat may have been poisoned and being able to quickly contact the right people could save your cat's life.

Toxic Cleaning Substances

If you keep toxic cleaning substances (including fertilizers, vermin or snail poisons and vehicle products) in your home, garage or garden shed, always keep them behind closed doors.

As well, keep any medications where your kitten or cat can never get to them and seriously consider eliminating the use of any and all toxic products, for the health of both yourself, your family and your best fur friends.

8. Why Does My Cat Eat Grass?

Be aware that many kittens and adult cats will eat grass for many reasons, such as when they need to purge the indigestible contents in their digestive tract or because they need more folic acid in their system, which helps with the production of hemoglobin.

There are also theories that the ingesting of a little grass acts as a natural cat laxative to help move fur balls through the digestive tract.

Remember that so long as the grass is healthy and has not been sprayed with toxic chemicals, a little grass eating should not be a concern.

9. Animal Poison Control Centers

The ASPCA Animal Poison Control Center is staffed 24 hours a day, 365 days a year and is a valuable resource for learning about what plants are toxic and possibly poisonous to your cat.

ASPCA Poison Control: www.aspca.org

a) USA Poison Emergency: Call: 1 (888) 426-4435

When calling the Poison Emergency number, your credit card may be charged with a $65 (£39.42) consultation fee.

b) UK Poison Emergency: Call: 0800-213-6680 - Pet Poison Helpline (payable service)

RSPCA: Call: 0300 1234 999

Chapter 19: Caring for Aging Cats

1. What to Be Aware Of

As a result of many modern advances in veterinarian care, improvements in diet and nutrition and general knowledge concerning proper care of our feline companions, our cats are often able to enjoy longer, healthier lives.

As such, when caring for our companions, we need to be aware of behavioral and physical changes that will affect our cats as they approach old age.

While each cat's individual health, genetics, and spirit will affect how old they seem and they may remain quite playful and active as they get older, most cats will be entering their senior years at around 7 years of age.

a) Physiological Changes: as our beloved companions enter into their late senior or geriatric years, they may be suffering from very similar physical aging problems that affect us humans, such as pain, stiffness and arthritis, and inability to control their bowels and bladder, which may reduce a cat's willingness to want to exercise.

b) Behavioral Changes: a senior cat may experience behavioral changes resulting from loss of hearing and sight, such as disorientation, fear or startle reactions and overall grumpiness from any number of physical problems that could be causing them pain whenever they move.

Just as research and science has improved our human quality of life in our senior years, the same is becoming true for our feline counterparts, who are able to benefit from dietary supplements and pharmaceutical products to help them be as comfortable as possible as they age.

Of course, there will be some inconveniences associated with keeping a cat with advancing years around the home, however, your cat deserves no less than to spend their final days in your loving care.

c) Geriatric Cats: being aware of the changes that are occurring in a senior cat will help you to better care for them during their geriatric years.

For instance, most cats will experience hearing loss and visual impairment and how you help them will depend upon which goes first (hearing or sight).

If a cat's hearing is compromised, then you will need to be aware that deaf cats will still be able to hear louder noises and feel vibrations, therefore hand clapping, knocking on walls, doors or furniture, using a loud clicker or stomping your foot on the floor may be a way to get their attention.

If a senior cat loses their eyesight, he or she will still be able to easily navigate their familiar surroundings and a cat that has been used to freedom in the great outdoors may have to be confined to staying home, perhaps only wandering in the back yard under your supervision.

If they still have their hearing, you will be able to assist your cat with verbal cues and commands. Cats that have lost both their hearing and their sight will need to be close to you, so that they can relax and not feel nervous and so that you can communicate by touching parts of their body.

Generally speaking, even when a cat becomes blind and/or deaf, their sense of smell may still be functioning, which means that they will be able to smell where you are and navigate their environment by using their nose.

d) More Bathroom Breaks: you may begin to notice that trips to the litter box or toilet are becoming more frequent in older cats who may lose their ability to hold it for longer periods of time. So, be prepared to be more watchful in case they are having difficulties getting into the litter box or balancing on the toilet.

Our beloved feline companions may also begin to show signs of cognitive decline and changes in the way their brain functions (similar to what happens to humans suffering from Alzheimer's), where they start to wander about aimlessly, sometimes during the middle of the night.

If your senior cat is wandering at night, make sure that they cannot accidentally fall down stairs or harm themselves in any way.

Being aware that an aging cat will be experiencing many symptoms that are similar to an aging human will help you to understand how best to keep them safe and as comfortable as possible during this golden time in their lives.

2. How to Make Them Comfortable

a) Regular Check-ups: during this time in your cat's life, when their immune systems become weakened and they may be experiencing pain, you will want to get into the habit of taking your senior cat for regular veterinarian check-ups.

Take them for a check-up every six months so that early detection of any problems can quickly be attended to and solutions for helping to keep your aging friend comfortable can be provided.

b) No Rough Play: an older cat will not have the same energy or willingness to play that they did when they were younger, therefore, do not allow younger children to rough house with an older cat.

Explain that the cat is getting older and that as a result they must learn to be gentle and to leave the cat alone when it may want to rest or sleep.

c) Mild Exercise: even aging cats may still enjoy a little game, even when they are getting older and slowing down. Although an older cat will generally have less energy, they still need to exercise and keep moving and taking the time to play their favorite games will keep them healthier and happier long into old age.

d) Best Quality Food: everyone has heard the saying, *"you are what you eat"* and for a senior cat, what he or she eats is even more important as his or her digestive system may no longer be functioning at peak performance.

Therefore, feeding high quality, protein-based food will be important for a senior cat's continued health.

As well, if your older cat is overweight, you will want to help them shed excess pounds so that they will not be placing undue stress on their joints or heart. The best way to accomplish this is by establishing a regular feeding routine and offering smaller quantities of a higher quality food.

e) Clean and Parasite Free: the last thing an aging cat should have to deal with is the misery of itching and scratching, so make sure that you continue to ensure they are free from biting bugs.

f) Plenty of Water: proper hydration is essential for helping to keep an older cat comfortable.

Water is life giving for every creature, so make certain that your aging cat has easy access to plenty of clean, fresh water which will help to improve their energy and digestion and also prevent dehydration which can add to joint stiffness.

g) Keep Them Warm: just as older humans feel the cold more, so do older cats. Keeping your senior cat warm will help to alleviate some of the pain of their joint stiffness or arthritis.

Make sure their bed or kennel is not kept in a drafty location and perhaps consider a heated bed for them. Be aware that your aging cat will be more sensitive to extremes in temperature and it will be up to you to make sure that they are comfortable at all times, which means not too hot and not too cold.

h) Steps or Stairs: if your cat is allowed to sleep on the human couch or chair but they are having difficulties getting up there (as their joints are becoming stiff and painful), consider buying or making them a set of soft, foam stairs so that they do not have to make the jump to their favourite sleeping place.

i) Comfortable Bed: while most cats seem to find the best place to sleep (which is usually up higher than the floor), providing a raised padded, soft bed will greatly help to relieve sore spots and joint pain in older cats.

If there is a draft in the home, generally it will be at floor level and therefore, a bed that is raised up off of the floor will be warmer for your senior cat.

j) More Love and Attention: last, but not least, make sure that you give your senior cat lots of love and attention, because when they are not feeling their best, they will want to be with you all that much more because you are their trusted guardian.

3. What is Euthanasia?

Every veterinarian will have received special training to help provide all incurably ill, injured or aged pets that have come to the end of their natural lives with a humane and gentle death, through a process called *"euthanasia"*.

When the time comes, euthanasia, or putting a cat *"to sleep"*, will usually be a two-step process.

First, the veterinarian will inject the cat with a sedative to make them sleepy, calm and comfortable and then, the veterinarian will inject a special drug that will peacefully stop their heart.

These drugs work in such a way that the cat will not experience any awareness whatsoever that his or her life is transitioning toward a peaceful ending. What they will experience is very much like what we humans experience when falling asleep under anesthesia during a surgical procedure.

Once the second stage drug has been injected, the entire process takes about 10 to 20 seconds, at which time the veterinarian will then check to make certain that the cat's heart has stopped.

There is no suffering with this process, which is a very gentle and humane way to end a cat's suffering and allow them to peacefully pass on.

4. When to Help a Cat Transition

The impending loss of a beloved cat is one of the most painfully difficult and emotionally devastating experiences their human guardian will ever have to face.

For the sake of our faithful companions (because we do not want to prolong their suffering), we humans will have to do our best to look at our cat's situation practically, rather than emotionally, so that we can make the best decision for them.

They may be suffering from extreme old age and the inability to even walk to their bathroom to relieve themselves means having to deal with the indignity of regularly soiling their sleeping area. They may have been diagnosed with an incurable illness that is causing them much pain or they may have been seriously injured.

Whatever the reason for a feline companion's suffering, it will be up to their human guardian to calmly guide the end-of-life experience, so that any further discomfort and distress can be minimized.

5. What to Do If You Are Uncertain

In circumstances where it is not entirely clear how much a cat is suffering, it will be helpful to pay close attention to your cat's behavior and keep a daily log or record, so that you can know for certain how much of their day is difficult and painful for them.

When you keep a daily log, it will be easier to decide if the cat's quality of life has become so poor that it makes better sense to offer them the gift of peacefully going to sleep.

During this time of uncertainty, it will also be very important to discuss with your veterinarian what signs of suffering may be associated with the cat's particular disease or condition, so that you know what to look for.

Often a cat may still continue to eat or drink despite being upset, having difficulty breathing, being disoriented or in much pain. As their caring guardian, you will have to weigh how much you love them and want them to stay with you against how much they may be really suffering in all other aspects of their life.

Obviously, if you can clearly see that your beloved companion is suffering throughout their days and nights, it will make sense to help humanely end their suffering by planning a euthanasia procedure.

We humans are often tempted to delay the inevitable moment of euthanasia, because we love our cats so much and cannot bear the anticipation of the intense grief we know will overwhelm us when we must say our final goodbyes to our beloved fur friend.

Unfortunately, we may regret that we allowed our cat to suffer too long and could find ourselves wishing that we gave them the gift of peacefully crossing over the Rainbow Bridge much sooner.

6. Grieving a Lost Friend

Some humans do not fully recognize the terrible grief involved in losing a beloved feline friend. There will be many who do not understand the close bond we humans can have with our cats, which is often unlike any we have with our human counterparts.

Your friends may give you pitying looks and try to cheer you up, but if they have never experienced such a loss themselves, they may also secretly think that you are making too much fuss over "just a cat".

For some of us humans, the loss of a beloved cat is so painful that we decide never to share our lives with another, because we cannot bear the thought of going through the pain of loss again.

Expect to feel terribly sad, tearful and yes, depressed because those who are close to their feline companions will feel their loss no less acutely than the loss of a human friend or life partner. The grieving process can take some time to recover from, and some of us never totally recover.

After the loss of a family cat, first you need to take care of yourself by making certain that you keep eating and getting regular sleep, even though you will feel an almost eerie sense of loneliness.

Losing a beloved cat is a serious shock to the system, which can also affect your concentration and your ability to find joy or want to participate in other activities that may be part of your daily life.

During this early grieving time, you will need to take extra care while driving or performing tasks that require your concentration as you may find yourself distracted.

If there are other cats or pets in the home, they will also be grieving the loss of a companion and may display this by acting depressed, being off their food or showing little interest in play or games. Therefore, you need to help guide your other pets through this grieving process by keeping them busy and interested, and spending more time with them.

Many people do not wait long enough before attempting to replace a lost pet and will immediately go to the local shelter and rescue a deserving cat. While this may help to distract you from your grieving process, this is not really fair to the new fur member of your family.

Bringing a new pet into a home where everyone is depressed and grieving the loss of a long time feline member may create behavioral problems for the new cat, who will be faced with learning all about their new home while also dealing with the unstable, sad energy of the grieving family.

A better scenario would be to allow yourself the time to properly grieve by waiting a minimum of one month to allow yourself and your family to feel happier and more stable before deciding upon sharing your home with another cat.

The grieving process will be different for everyone and you will know when the time is right to consider sharing your home with another feline companion.

7. The Rainbow Bridge Poem

The Rainbow Bridge poem (written by an unknown author) has given hope and solace to many when they are grieving the loss of a fur friend and there may come a time when it will help you to feel less stressed over the loss of a dear companion.

<u>Rainbow Bridge</u>

"Just this side of heaven is a place called Rainbow Bridge.

When an animal dies that has been especially close to someone here, that pet goes to Rainbow Bridge.

There are meadows and hills for all of our special friends, so they can run and play together.

There is plenty of food, water and sunshine, and our friends are warm and comfortable.

All animals who had been ill and old are restored to health and vigor;

Those who were hurt or maimed are made whole and strong again,
just as we remember them in our dreams of days and times gone by.

The animals are happy and content, except for one small thing;
they each miss someone very special to them, who had to be left
behind.

They all run and play together,
but the day comes when one suddenly stops
and looks into the distance.
His bright eyes are intent; His eager body quivers.

Suddenly he begins to run from the group,
flying over the green grass, his legs carrying him faster and faster.

You have been spotted,
and when you and your special friend finally meet,
you cling together in joyous reunion, never to be parted again.

The happy kisses rain upon your face; your hands again caress the
beloved head and you look once more into the trusting eyes
of your pet, so long gone from your life

but never absent from your heart.

Then you cross Rainbow Bridge together...."

8. Memorials

There are as many ways to honor the passing of a beloved cat, as each
of our furry friends is uniquely special to us.

For instance, you and your family may wish to have your companion
cremated and preserve their ashes in a special urn that you would keep
in a place of honor, or sprinkle their ashes in the flower bed, or under a
favorite tree they liked to climb.

Perhaps you will want to have a special marker, photo bereavement,
painting, photo engraved Rainbow Bridge Poem, or wooden plaque
created in honor of your passed friend.

Those who have been very close to their beloved fur friend may choose to keep their memory really close to them at all times by having a DNA remembrance pendant or bracelet designed.

As well, there are support groups, such as Rainbow Bridge, which is a grief support community to help you and your family through this painful period of loss and grief.

Chapter 20: Scottish Fold Cat Adoption

When you are considering rescuing and adopting a specific breed of cat or kitten, the first place to begin your search will be your local breeders, shelters and rescue groups.

There are many breed-specific rescue organizations in Canada, the USA, the United Kingdom and many other countries and the easiest way to find one closest to you is to go online and type in the breed name of the cat you want to rescue next to the name of the city where you live.

1. Shelters and Rescues

Here you can expect to pay an adoption fee to cover the cost of spaying or neutering, but this will be only a small percentage of what you would pay a breeder and you will be saving a life at the same time.

Adopt a Pet (online): *"...is North America's largest non-profit pet adoption website. We help over 13,600 animal shelters, humane societies, SPCAs, pet rescue groups and pet adoption agencies advertise their homeless pets to millions of adopters a month, for free. We're all about getting homeless pets into homes..."*

Blue Cross For Pets: *"...We find homes for unwanted cats, dogs, small pets and horses across the UK and our tailor-made service means we help each pet find the right person for them..."*

Cat Cuddles Sanctuary: *"...Cat Cuddles is a registered charity that is all about promoting and strengthening the feline-human bond and helping pair up unwanted cats with loving forever homes and humans. The charity receives no funding from state or grants.*

Our sustainability and success as a charity are entirely based on the goodwill of our donors, continuous interest of key supporters and the selfless dedication, hard work and passion of the volunteer team..."

Specialty Purebred Cat Rescue: *"...Specialty Purebred Cat Rescue is a non-profit organization founded in 1999. We specialize in finding quality homes for abandoned/surrendered purebred cats. We are the largest rescue organization of its kind in the Midwest and we are well known and respected throughout the animal shelter community.*

Our mission is to use our specialized knowledge of cat breeds to provide an appropriate foster alternative for homeless purebred cats and kittens whose special requirements are difficult to meet in a shelter environment, in addition to helping as many special needs domestic cats as our resources allow..."

Cats Protection: *"...is the United Kingdom's leading feline welfare charity. Our vision is a world where every cat is treated with kindness and an understanding of its needs.*

It's an ambitious vision. However, we truly believe it can be achieved because of our passion, our professional approach and simply because cats are among the UK's most popular companion pets..."

2. Online Resources

Sites such as Petango, Adopt A Pet and Pet Finder can be good places to begin your search. Each of these online resources is a central gathering site for hundreds and hundreds of local shelters, humane societies and rescue groups.

3. Feline Clubs and Breeders

Another place to search will be clubs or breeders in your local area. These groups may have rescue cats available or may be able to recommend a reputable breeder in your area.

Chapter 21: Resources & References

The following resources and references are listed alphabetically within their specific category and include web addresses.

1. Poison Control

ASPCA Poison Control: www.aspca.org

Poisonous Plants Affecting Animals - Cornell University, Department of Animal Science: www.ansci.cornell.edu/plants

2. Breeders, Associations & Rescues

Adopt A Pet: www.adoptapet.com

Albafold: www.abafold.com

American Cat Fanciers Association: www.acfacat.com

Blue Cross for Pets: www.bluecross.org.uk

Cat Cuddles: www.catcuddles.org.uk

Cat Fanciers' Association: www.cfa.org

Cats Protection: www.cats.org.uk

Kittens For Adoption: www.kittensforadoption.co.uk

Lukaraza: www.lukaraza.com

Pets 4 Homes: www.pets4homes.co.uk

Petango: petango.com

Pet Finder: www.petfinder.com

Purr-fect Folds Cattery: www.purrfect-folds.com

The International Cat Association: www.tica.org

The Governing Council of the Cat Fancy: www.gccfcats.org

Wunderfoldes Scottish Fold Cattery: www.wunderfolds.com

3. Equipment

Amazingly Cat: www.amazinglycat.com

Bespoke Cat Runs: www.woodenart.org.uk

Catio Spaces: www.catiospaces.com

CitiKitty: www.citikitty.com

Litter Kwitter: www.litterkwitter.com

Poochie Bells: http://poochie-pets.net/

Sleepy Pod: sleepypod.com

Tell Bell: tellbell.com

Tick Twister: www.ticktwister.com

ThunderShirt: www.thundershirt.com

4. Supplies

Amazingly Cat: www.amazinglycat.com

Better Way Cat Litter: www.ultrapet.com

CedarCide: www.cedarcide.com

Cedarific Natural Cat Litter: www.cedarific.com

Eco-Shell's Purr and Simple Cat Litter: www.greenlittlecat.com

Feline Pine: www.felinepine.com

Pet Protector: www.petprotector.org

Remove Urine Odors: www.removeurineodors.com

Swheat Scoop Natural Wheat Litter: www.swheatscoop.com

World's Best Cat Litter: www.worldsbestcatlitter.com

Yesterday's News Cat Litter: www.yesterdaysnewcatlitter.com

5. Services

Knows To Nose: www.knowstonose.com

Must Have Publishing: www.musthavepublishing.com

Tattoo-A-Pet: www.tattoo-a-pet.com/

6. Resources

The Truth About Pet Cancer: www.thetruthaboutpetcancer.com

7. Memorials

Rainbow Bridge: www.rainbowsbridge.com/

Published by Worldwide Information Publishing 2018

Made in the USA
Columbia, SC
04 October 2023

23916318R00104